Peculiar Favor

Accidental Thoughts on God's Grace

by Charlie Jones

JavAgapé Press
Franklin, TN

Peculiar Favor

Copyright © 2003 JavAgapé Press
by Charlie Jones

Published by
JavAgapé Press
4008 Oxford Glen Dr.
Suite 301
Franklin, TN 37067

Cover Photo by
David Sacks Photography
New York, NY
212.929.9382
www.davidsacks.com

ISBN 0-9740747-0-5

Printed in the United States of America
1st printing

For everyone there is that special memory of delight: a Christmas, a "first date," a warm gathering of family, a rustic picnic in the woods, the first smell of coffee in the morning. These delights and special joys define us and shape our perspectives on Life.

I am fortunate enough to live with a person who embodies all the delights and joys I could ever hope for. She is my memory-maker and my best friend. She is the most talented person I have ever met. Ruth is my partner and fellow traveler on the road of Grace.

I dedicate this book, my life and my heart to my wife, Ruth.

Table of Contents

Acknowledgements

I am indebted to so many for the thoughts and experiences in this book, I hardly know where to begin. But then again perhaps many of these people would feel better if NOT acknowledged by a peculiar person like me. Nevertheless, I will mention them for they have my thanks and my love.

To begin in the beginning, I want to thank Dr. Richard Pratt who taught me more theology than anyone else in my life. During the Jesus Movement (thirty years ago!!!!), Richard and I were converted to Christ at the same time. Richard was a freak and I was a "wanna be" freak. He held Bible studies and fellowships practically every night. It was during these Bible studies that I learned the Doctrines of Grace and was taught how to properly read, weigh, and consider the Word of God. These principles of hermeneutics and this foundation of thought have guided me all my life. Thank you, Richard.

Second, I want to thank Dr. Jack Miller. Jack taught me more of grace and forgiveness than anyone else in my life. It was Jack who brought the good news of Gospel singing into my heart. After much sin and horror, I was convinced that God was "gonna git me." It was through Jack's ministry that I learned of the loving Father who scans the horizon seeking the prodigal son, anticipating the party of forgiveness. I could also relate to Jack, for he too had been a member of the frozen chosen, but then had been thawed-out in the warmth of Light.

I would also like to thank: Dave McCarty, who counseled me through my beginning years in grace; Paul Miller, whose illustrations and thought-provoking examples from his own life, gave me courage to look honestly at myself; Rose Ann

Trott, who God used to provide a break-through in my stubborn heart; Rose Marie Miller, who taught me to see my life as God's canvas and how to pay closer attention to His brush strokes; Clyde Godwin, who prayed with me and showed me grace through a very difficult time of life–even while he was going through his own difficulties.

I would also like to express my undying love and appreciation for Steve Brown. I have often told people, "Jack Miller taught me about grace, but Steve Brown gave me permission." Steve, your courage to be real and your honesty about your wrestling match with God has inspired me over and over again. You are a precious jewel in my life. Thanks for being who you are and for being so lavish in your love toward me.

There are dozens more and I hope they will forgive me for not mentioning them. But these are the people who did the most to make me realize that, indeed, I stand "smack-dab" in the middle of God's Peculiar Favor. What a life I have been given! What a group of friends and lovers!

God bless you all.

Peculiar Favor
Accidental Thoughts On God's Grace

Preface

Why write yet another book on GRACE? Well, for one thing, I want to make some money. Second, I want to feel important. Very important. Third, I have some of THE best thoughts ever on the subject–all others are inferior to mine. And oh, yeah, the fourth thing, I want to prove that God can work through strange people with bad, selfish, even sinful, motives (see reasons 1-3 above). Of course, there are several more bad motives and reasons that I haven't listed above, but I do hope you understand: this book is about God's favor for those people who don't deserve it–of which, I am the chief.

Most of us would immediately agree that no one deserves God's favor, yet in our Evangelical sub-culture we go to great lengths trying to prove to God, ourselves and others that, while we didn't deserve God's grace at one time in our lives, we certainly do now. We may not articulate it in these terms but this is the way we live our lives. This is why we pretend to be better than we are. This is why we don't "come clean" with one another and confess our sins. This is why the church is so scandalized when true sinners are found in its midst. As I write this, the news networks are squawking out the story of a Christian school in the mid-west which kicked-out a kindergarten student because it found out that her mother was a stripper. Something tells me that the Author and Perfecter of our Faith, would be the first one to show compassion not only to this little girl, but to her stripper mother as well. But in today's Disneyland of Christianity, we MUST maintain our witness and get rid of any "real sinners" in our midst. This is why the World looks at us in the Church and wonders "What have they been smokin'?"

We talk love and forgiveness yet these are rare commodities in many of our churches. Many of us in the Christian sub-culture live as if there were no true love and no true forgiveness. So many of us are worn to a frazzle by guilt and depressed that we are not better Christians. We burn with anger and resentment toward that brother or sister who wronged us. Do we start new churches because so many non-christians are brought to the Lord? No, it is because so many Christians cannot stand the thought of worshiping with some set of other Christians who have risen up in their midst. We start denominations because so many of us cannot get along. Our pride, anger, unbelief and rage rule the day. Veins bulge, knuckles whiten, ears burn and daggers are thrown… all in the name of the One who said that others will know we are His disciples by the peculiar love we have for one another.

Lest I be accused of hypocrisy (yet hypocrisy seems to be a favorite sin of mine), let me be quick to say that I am in the above group. I am selfish, self-centered, easily angered, controlling, lustful, vengeful, unforgiving and just plain mean. That is why it is important that I write a book about grace. If I found a place at the Table of Wonder, then there has to be room for you too. Therefore, come fellow traveler, let's go together into the realms of Glory, the Kingdom of God's Smile, and see what is available for us.

The title has been through several revisions. I had several spiffy ideas but kept coming back to Peculiar Grace. But then I got to looking at all the books on the market about grace and decided that I didn't want to be a "me too" in this field so I settled on the other word that most closely signifies God's grace and that is God's favor. Now we come to the subtitle and this is what I want to explain. I purposely interjected the word "accidental" to be honest with you about my life with God. And my skills as an organizer. I am an artist and a right-brain kind o' guy. There are very, very few things in my life that are purposeful and planned. Anything that I have learned about God I have learned through a series of Divine "accidents." At least that's how it always seems to me at the time. But of course, as I know, my life is in His hands and what seems accidental to me is divinely planned and protected by His almighty arms. So if you are a scattered, right-brain person and your life seems to be a mess much more than it seems to be a success, then take cheer. There are others out there, like me, who suffer from the same sense of "failure" yet have turned to see the smile of Christ.

Also the word "accidental" gives you a hint about how to use this book. There is no beginning, middle or end. Read this book at your leisure and in any order. Each section follows a certain theme but most chapters are self-contained.

I also had the notion of calling this the first ever Bathroom Reader on Grace. The chapters are short and can be read in a single "sitting." Just put it in the appropriate place and enjoy while you take care of other business. Or as my friend Annie says, "It is the only multi-tasking that men are capable of performing."

Welcome to my heart, mind and life with God. I hope you will have as much fun reading this as I have had in writing it. God bless and happy travels.

Charlie Jones
May 2002

Foreword

I have a horrible tendency to forget important stuff like birthdays, anniversaries and holidays. It may be because I'm getting older but, given that I've always forgotten important stuff, it's probably just intrinsic to who I am.

However there is a forgetfulness that is common and intrinsic to every Christian. It is a part of the fall and Christians must fight it all the time. We forget how good the good news really is. Paul was surprised when the Galatians forgot. He wrote: "O foolish Galatians! Who has bewitched you?... Are you so foolish? Having begun by the Spirit, are you now being perfected by the flesh?" In other words: What were you thinking?

Paul should not have been surprised. We can't help it.

There is something in us that causes us to become the very thing Jesus came to prevent. Maybe we believe that we could not be that bad or that God's grace could be that good. Maybe it's just that a religion of rules and righteousness is attractive because we want to do it ourselves and, more importantly, get the credit for it. It could be that pride and self-righteousness are so much a part of us that we're attracted to that which affirms it. And then it could be that we've been playing the game of religion for so long that we're used to it and perhaps believe that it is the only game in town.

When Karl Barth wrote his commentary on Romans, someone said that he had "thrown a bomb into the playground of the liberals." Sometimes "bombs" need to be thrown into playgrounds. Charlie Jones has thrown a "bomb" into the playground of the self-righteousness, the legalists and the very religious folks. That can hurt. Believe me, I know because I'm one of them.

But it is a hurt that heals. This is a book that will set you free and teach you to dance. It is a book about truth, about love, about freedom, about grace… and more importantly, a book about Jesus.

Charlie Jones is one of the most intense and gifted guys I know. Don't let his humor fool you. This is a very serious book about a very serious subject. Charlie, like the rest of us, is drawn to the religion of "trying harder." And, frankly, if anybody could pull it off, it would be Charlie. He can't… and I'm so glad. Because in his failure, and his honesty about it, there is a powerful message of grace and freedom.

In his On the Freedom of the Christian, Martin Luther wrote:

> I believe that it has now become clear that it is not enough or in any sense "Christian" to preach the works, life, and words of Christ… as if the knowledge of these would suffice for the conduct of life… Yet, this is the fashion among those who today [1500's] are regarded as our best preachers… and such teaching is childish and effeminate nonsense.
> Rather ought Christ to be preached to the end that faith in him may be established that he may not only be Christ, but be Christ for you and me, and that which is said of him and is denoted in his name may be effectual in us. Such faith is produced and preserved in us by preaching why Christ came, what he brought and bestowed, what benefit it is to us to accept him… What person is there whose heart, upon hearing these things, will not rejoice to its depth and when receiving such comfort will not grow tender so that they will love Christ as they never could by means of any law or work?
> There are some who have no understanding to hear the truth of freedom and insist upon their goodness as means for salvation. These people you must resist, do the very opposite, and offend them boldly lest by their impious views they drag many with them into error. For the sake of

liberty of the faith do other things which they regarded as the greatest of sins… use your freedom constantly and consistently in the sight of and despite the tyrants and stubborn so that they may learn that they are impious, that their law and works are of no avail for righteousness, and that they had no right to set them up.

This is an earthy and honest book that does what Martin Luther said we ought to do, to wit, offend "boldly" those who can't bear those who teach the whole counsel of God regarding our sin and God's grace.

Read this book…laugh, sing and dance in the presence of One who loves you far more than you could ever understand.

If you're offended, I'm so sorry. I'll pray for you.

There is something so sad about people who don't know the song, don't get the joke and have never learned to dance.

Steve Brown
"Big Kahuna" Seminary Prof
Reformed Theological Seminary
Radio Personality
President, Key Life Ministries
Anna's Husband

INTRODUCTION

Much of what I know about God's favor for me has sprung from the jovial madman Martin Luther. It was Luther's boldness and devil-may-care attitude that enthralled me from the beginning of my transformation from elder brother to prodigal son.

Since Luther provided the foundation of my thoughts on the wonder of God's favor I wanted you to hear it "from the horse's mouth." Below you will find his preface to the book of Galatians Every time I read it I am astounded by the beauty of the Gospel of Christ. Read this now and read it whenever you feel alone. By the way, all subtitles and bold emphasis are mine.

Martin Luther's Argument of the Epistle of St. Paul to the Galatians

A Transliteration by Rev. Bill Slack

Paul sets down the biblical teachings of faith, grace, forgiveness of sins or Christian righteousness, so that we can know without a doubt the difference between "Christian" righteousness and all other kinds of righteousness. There is political or civil righteousness that the world leaders, philosophers and lawyers deal with. There's ceremonial righteousness (acting correctly at weddings or formal dinners, etc.) that deals with men's tradition. This righteousness parents and teachers can teach safely, because they don't claim that being righteous in these ways pays for sin or makes us perfect or pleases God or earns us God's favor, but they teach these righteous ways to correct our manners and teach us about our day-to-day life with other people. There is another type of righteousness called the "righteousness of the law" or the Ten Commandments, that Moses teaches. The church teaches about this too but in light of faith.

The better righteousness

There is another far better righteousness that is, "righteousness of faith" or "Christian righteousness." This righteousness we must separate from the rest because they work in a completely opposite way to Christian righteousness. The other kinds of righteousness come out of the laws of governments (we obey the law and are righteous) or church tradition or even the Ten Commandments. The other kinds of righteousness we can work at ourselves by our own strength or by extra strength that God gives us, because we couldn't even be righteous in these ways without God's strength. He gives all good things that we enjoy.

But this Christian righteousness is the greatest righteousness. God puts it on us without our lifting a finger. It's not political or ceremonial. It doesn't have to do with our obeying God's law. It has nothing to do with what we do or how hard we work, but it is given to us and we do nothing for it. It's "passive righteousness" where the others we have to work for. With this "free righteousness" we don't do anything, we don't give anything to God, but we receive and allow someone else to do all the work for us and in us, and it's God that does it. That's why we'll call it "passive righteousness."

This "passive righteousness" is a mystery that someone who doesn't know Jesus can't understand. As a matter of fact, Christians don't completely understand it and don't take advantage of it when they're tempted. So we have to constantly teach it over and over again to others and repeat it to ourselves, because if we don't understand it and have it in our hearts, we will be defeated by our enemy, and we'll be totally depressed. There is nothing that gives us peace like this "passive righteousness."

But men are so weak and miserable that when we are close to death or afraid of God, we do not see anything but what we have done to be righteous, how worthy we have made ourselves, and the Law (The Ten Commandments). And when we see the Law, we see our sin and the evil in our lives comes to mind, and it tears us apart, and we groan and think, "How bad I have been; my life is full of hate and evil. Please, God let me live and I will fix up what I have done wrong." So, man is so evil that all he can see is what he should do to be righteous. He is so evil that he cannot see what Christ has done for him to be righteous.

The conscience: Gospel freedom & Satan's target

On the other side, Satan, taking advantage of our natural weakness, increases and fires up those thoughts in us. Then our consciences are more troubled, terrified and confused. For it is impossible for a man's mind by itself to find comfort, look for God's grace, or reject Satan's argument about works just because he feels sinful and is disgusted by it. These things are far above man's strength and ability; in fact, it's even beyond the power of God's law. It is true that God's law is the most excellent thing in the world, but it is not able to ease a man's troubled conscience, rather it increases his fear and causes him to despair; "that through the commandment sin might become utterly sinful." (Rom. 7:18)

So the afflicted and troubled conscience has no cure for

17

desperation and death unless it takes hold of the forgiveness of sins by grace, offered free of charge in Jesus Christ, that is "Christian" or "passive" righteousness. When the person realizes this, he is at peace and can say "I am not going to work for my righteousness, even though I need to have it, and I need to be righteous. Because even if I could work up to righteousness and fulfill what I thought was righteousness, still I could not trust it to make me right at the judgement of God. So I throw away all my works, my tries at obeying God's law, and firmly hold on to "passive righteousness," that is the righteousness of grace, mercy and the forgiveness of sins. In short, I trust only in the righteousness that Christ and the Holy Spirit give me!!

It is like this, the earth does not produce rain, nor is it able by its own power or work to get it. The earth simply receives it as a gift of God from above. It is the same with "passive" righteousness; it is given to us by God without our deserving it or working for it. So let's look at what the earth is able to do to get the rain each season so that it can be fruitful, and we will see how much we are able in our own strength and works to do to get heavenly and eternal righteousness. We see we will never be able to attain it unless God Himself, by the great gift of His Son, gives us Jesus' perfect record, and gives us Jesus' perfect righteousness. The greatest knowledge and wisdom a Christian can have then is, not to know the Law, but to forget works and to forget all our working toward righteousness, especially when we think about God judging us. The person that does not know Christ, on the other hand, needs to know and earnestly seek the Law and good works.

But it is a very strange thing, and unknown to the world, to teach Christians not to know the Law, and to live before God as if there were no Law or wrath of God, but total grace and mercy for Christ's sake! But even though it is strange, unless one disregards the Law and is convinced in his own heart that there is no Law or wrath from God but only grace and mercy for Christ's sake, he cannot be saved because all the Law does is show us our sin.

On the other hand, works and keeping of the Law must be required in the world as if there were no promise of grace because people are stubborn, proud, and hardhearted, and they need only the Law put in front of their faces so that they will be terrified and humbled. The Law is given to terrify and kill the proud, stubborn man and tear out his old nature, and both the word of grace and wrath must be rightly understood according to Paul. (2 Tim. 2)

The Law and Gospel

A faithful and wise preacher or teacher of the Word will give out the Law in such a way that it is kept in perspective. The man that teaches that people are justified before God by obeying the Law gives the Law much more power than it has and mixes up the "passive righteousness" with "learned righteousness." He is a bad teacher because he misunderstands the Word. On the other hand, he that uses the Law to cause a man to see his sinfulness and convict him yet also shows how God forgives sin (by "passive righteousness") teaches the Word well. This is how the man repents and turns from that sin, for the man that does not know Christ must be shown the Law and works. The new man (one who knows Christ) must be affirmed in God's promises and mercy. So when I see a man that is bruised enough already, burdened by the Law, terrified with sin, and thirsting for relief, that is when, in truth, it is time to take the Law and "works" of righteousness out of his sight and show him, by the Gospel, "passive righteousness" (Christian righteousness) which offers the promise of Christ without the Law; that Christ came for the hurting and for sinners. Then the man is raised up and has good hope, he is no longer under the Law but covered by grace. How is he out from under the Law? Because he is a new man to whom the Law does not apply!! For the Law does not reach past Christ as Paul says, "Christ is the end of the Law." (Rom. 10:4) Since Christ has come, Moses' Law ends, circumcision ends, the sacrifices, the sabbaths, yes, even all the prophets end.

This is our goal, that we teach how to show the difference between the two kinds of righteousness, "works" and "passive," to the end that outward actions and faith, works and grace, policy and religion should not be confused and mixed together or taken for the other. Both are necessary, but both must be kept in their bounds. Christian or "passive righteousness" only applies to the new man (one who knows Christ), and "works" righteousness only applies to the old man, who is born only of flesh and blood. Upon the old man, as upon a donkey, a great load must be placed to press him down, and until he becomes a new man by faith in Christ, he cannot know the Spirit of grace and enjoy the Kingdom, both of which we are able to appreciate now and in the fullness of the Lord's grace to come.

This I say so that no man thinks we reject or forbid good works, as the Papists falsely accuse us, because they don't understand what they are saying themselves or what we teach. They only know the righteousness of the Law ("works" righteousness). Yet they pass judgement on the doctrine of "passive righteousness" which is above the Law and which no carnal man is able to judge. That is why they are offended; they can't see any higher than the Law. Whatever is higher than the Law then is a great offense to them. But we have in our minds two worlds, one heavenly, the other earthly. We put these two kinds of righteousness ("works" and "passive") in these two worlds being set far apart from each other. The righteousness of the Law (works) is earthly and has to do with earthly things, and by it we do good works. But just like the earth does not bring forth fruit unless it is first watered and made fruitful from above, even so by "works" righteousness, by doing many things, we do nothing. And in obeying the Law, we do not really obey it unless first (without deserving it or working for it) we are made righteous by the Christian (passive) righteousness, which has nothing to do with "works" righteousness of the Law or to earthly righteousness. But this righteousness is heavenly; which as we said, we do not do it ourselves, but receive it from heaven. We don't work for it, but by grace it is given to us, and we get it through faith. It takes us above the Law and works. So as we have looked and acted like, as Paul says, the earthly Adam, let us now look and act as the new man with a heavenly image in a new world where there is no Law, no sin, no guilt or pain in our conscience, no death, but perfect joy, righteousness, grace, peace, life, salvation, and glory.

So we do nothing? Don't we do any work to obtain this righteousness? I answer, nothing at all, for this is perfect righteousness; "to do nothing, to hear nothing, to know nothing of the Law or of works," but to know and believe only this, that Christ is gone to the Father and is not now seen. He sits at His Father's right hand not as a judge but making us, before God, wise, righteous, holy and redeemed; briefly, that He is our high Priest pleading for us and reigning over us and in us by grace. In this heavenly righteousness sin can have no place because there is no Law, and where there is no Law, there can be no breaking of the Law. (Rom. 4:15)

You see then that sin has no place here, so there can be no painful guilt, no fear, no weight on our shoulders. That is why John says (I John 5:18), "He that is born of God cannot sin." But if there is any fear or our conscience is bothered, it is a sign that our "passive righteousness" is 'withdrawn,' that is hidden from us, and Christ is darkened out of our sight. But when we truly see Christ, we have full and perfect joy in the Lord with peace of mind, and we certainly think: "Although I am a sinner by the law and under condemnation of the Law, still I don't despair, still I don't die, because Christ lives, who is both my righteousness and my everlasting life." In that righteousness and life I have no sin, no fear, no guilty conscience, no fear of death. I am indeed a sinner in this life of mine and in my own righteousness, as a child of Adam; where the Law accuses me, death controls me and eventually would destroy me. But I have another life, another righteousness above this life which is in Christ, the Son of God, who knows no sin or death but is eternal righteousness and eternal life; by Him this body of mine, being dead and turned to dust, shall be raised up again and freed from the chains of the Law and sin and shall be made holy together with the Spirit.

So we have both these (the old man and the new man) with us while we are here. The flesh is accused, tempted, weighed down with sorrow, bruised by the "works" of righteousness of the Law, but the Spirit reigns, rejoices and is saved by this "passive" and Christian righteousness, because our spirit knows that it has a Lord in heaven at the right hand of His Father who has done away with Law, sin, death, and has conquered all evil, captured it, and triumphed over it Himself. (Col 2:15)

...Jacob wrestled very hard with the angel, but he never won the victory till the angel touched the hollow of his thigh, and caused the sinew to shrink. Then, when Jacob could not any longer stand, as he fell, he clutched the angel with all his might as though he would pull him down also if he must himself go down, and the weight of Jacob was all the greater because he could not stand. His very weakness was an element of his strength, and that moment of weakness was the moment of his victory. ~C.H. Spurgeon

Chapter One

Life with God
Or the wrestling match that never ends

The year is 2000. The place is Rome, Italy. The mission is to bring Good News and refreshment to hundreds and thousands of visitors to Italy during the year of Jubilee for the Catholic Church. The translator is hired by Italy for Christ. Her name is Teresa, (pronounced Te-RAY-sa.) She is a former-Catholic turned Buddhist. She is a delight and frightfully hard working. She gets up early to study maps, arrange drop-off points, coordinate with ministry officials about the plans for the day, call restaurants and take care of the details needed to see our group through Italy. But there is a frustration about Teresa. She is full of life, full of emotion, full of facts and ideas, yet she is constantly frustrated by having to speak our language instead of her native tongue, Italian. She cannot speak well enough or think fast enough to say all that she wants to communicate. She is unable to convey all that is in her heart.

This seems to be a picture of my life with God. I have been hired by Him to be His. Yet it is my life's frustration that I cannot adequately ascend to the heights nor dredge from the depths all that I want to do, say or accomplish in God. I am constantly frustrated by my lack of skills in the spiritual realms.

Life with God (my life within His favor) has been a hearty mixture of excitement and frustration. While I find the wonders of grace and the forgiveness of Christ astounding, I am so frustrated with my limited abilities to grasp all that is there. I have heard someone say that trying to understand all that God has done for us in Christ is a bit like trying to take a sip of water from a gushing fire hydrant. I think this is true. I have also heard that Calvin said that the Scriptures are God's "baby talk" to us. And though He talks to us in "goo-goos and gaa-gaas" we still remain remarkably unable to grasp the spiritual side of life. We remain little more than infants and even baby talk seems to be awfully advanced for us. By the way, this why it is so amusing that we can still judge others for their lack of understanding. It is like a baby with wet diapers looking down in judgement on the infant who has soiled, messy diapers. In either circumstance, we are inadequate for life and need Another to come help us.

WWF & God & me

"This left Jacob all alone in the camp, and a man came and wrestled with him until dawn. When the man saw that he couldn't win the match, he struck Jacob's hip and knocked it out of joint at the socket. Then the man said, "Let me go, for it is dawn." But Jacob panted, "I will not let you go unless you bless me." "What is your name?" the man asked. He replied, "Jacob." "Your name will no longer be Jacob," the man told him. "It is now Israel, because you have struggled with both God and men and have won." "What is your name?" Jacob asked him. "Why do you ask?" the man replied. Then he blessed Jacob there. Jacob named the place Peniel–"face of God"–for he said, "I have seen God face to face, yet my life has been spared." The sun rose as he left Peniel, and he was limping because of his hip." Genesis 32:24-31, NLT.

Here stands my hero: a scoundrel of the highest sort; a liar, a cheat and a chicken, yet He recognizes the Holy when he sees Him and will not let Him go. He wrestles and strains with this strange alien being and finally is blessed because he will not let go of a good thing. And after his encounter with God, he rises to walk the rest of his life with a limp.

Do you identify with this saint? I do. I have spent my life grabbing onto this slippery celestial Being, holding on for dear life. In spite of my reluctance, my sins, my yearnings in the opposite direction, I am forever finding myself back in the match. The celestial SmackDown. The Trinitarian Tag Team match with my heart.

Many times we find ourselves weary with sweat, toil, blood and strain, yelling out in a primal scream, "I WILL NOT LET YOU GO UNLESS YOU BLESS ME!!!" True grit. The angst of the ages screamed into the black, dark hallway of faith. Then remarkably enough the dawn comes and we hear the blessing. Grace bestowed upon the sweaty, dirty mud wrestler.

We are Jacob. We are the liars and cheats of the world claiming a blessing we do not deserve. This is God's favor for those He loves. He pronounces the blessing and encourages us by saying that we have indeed seen the face of God and His face is smiling.

As a reminder of our blessing we also receive a curse of sorts– our blessing is capped-off with the affliction of a limp. A dislocated hip is our lifelong trophy for winning the wrestling match!

But wait. I thought grace was grace. How can I receive the blessing of God and still receive the affliction of a limp? In a materialistic, selfish world, the knowledge of God is an affliction. We become the crazy ones who walk funny. Our limp is obvious no matter where we walk, no matter what we do. Once we have wrestled with God, we are never the same and we never see the world in the same way again.

We will limp as we walk to the mirror and begin to truly see what is there. The mask begins to fade away and we begin to see the child of past fears, hurts and sorrow… and (for a change) we don't turn to run away. We begin to see the various coping mechanisms we have substituted for love and intimacy. Intimacy with God, intimacy with friends and intimacy with family. Our limp will remind us that we have wrestled with God therefore struggling with the mirror will not be as difficult as it once was.

Our limp will become obvious as we begin to see the "man behind the curtain" in our culture and in our lives. While all others are impressed with the smoke, fire, flash and thunder of Oz, we begin to see the charlatans who have distracted us from reality, the reality of grace. We not only see things differently. We also are seen as those different ones with that funny limp. But more about all this later. Suffice it to say that our encounters with God change us forever and the bolder we are in our encounter (I will not let go until you bless me.) the more profound the change.

Our limp is a sign, a remembrance, that we have been broken. It is the limp that will signal to other broken ones that we have been touched by the Holy and have lived to tell the tale. This limp attracts others in the midst of their wrestling match, hungry for strategy and relief. Yet the most profound relief we can give them is to tell the story of our own match with the Consuming Fire and how we lived to yet praise Him. We share our stories; we weep together; we laugh together. We become united in brokenness and in the glorious trophy of a God-given limp.

So don't be concerned that your life with God resembles much more of a wrestling match than the picture-perfect plan o' peace and pleasure that many say should be the norm for us as Christians. Be bold. Grab onto Him with all your might and hold on until He blesses you. It is only in the midst of struggle that 'peace' and 'pleasure' have any meaning.

Chapter Two

The Foundation Of Outrageous Thoughts

To talk about God and especially to talk about grace we must be accustomed to espousing outrageous statements. It's sort of like talking about UFO's. A person can't claim knowledge of alien creatures, green men or space abductions without sounding totally "out-of-it." The same should be true of us when we start talking about the Trinitarian God, who created the world from NOTHING, came down to live on earth with the determination of dying a horrible death; He rose from the dead, making several appearances including when he cooked breakfast for His friends. Then He ascended into the ozone and sent a supernatural Being called THE SPIRIT to live in weak, fearful humans. Now if none of that seems a bit far-out to you, then I would hate to attend your family reunions. The Addams family ain't got nothin' on you!

To me, every encounter with the Almighty in the

Scriptures has the feel of a good joke gone bad–or a bad joke gone good. The intrusion of the supernatural into the natural throws all common conversation out the window. It is outrageous. So in this chapter I would like to lay an outrageous foundation for all the other outrageous thoughts in this book.

The Gospel of peculiar favor

For many of us, "The Gospel" is the salvation message we heard years ago to which we made some response. Many may have walked down the aisle of a church at the invitation of the speaker. Some remember praying a prayer with someone. Still others changed their minds about the claims of Christ and simply believed. Nevertheless, we came to Christ and we all agree that it was through the Gospel message. However, for most of us the Gospel message is that fundamental, even childish (theologically) story of grace that brought us to the party, but it is not the "belle of the ball." We have long since forgotten the beauty of its message and have pursued more worthy escorts: theology, church, home schooling, witnessing, Bible study, good deeds, works-righteousness, more theology and daily devotions. As I was once fond of saying, "Enough milk, give me meat!" (I Cor. 3:1-2)

In the thirty years I have walked with Christ, I have come to see that the real meat of God's word is found in unpacking the profundity of the "simple" Gospel message. So when I talk of a love for the Gospel, I am speaking of an awe and devotion to this outrageous message: God loves me–mercy, justice and righteousness kiss one another in Jesus Christ. These simple statements will be the subject of every song, every story and every conversation when we are in Heaven. So I feel that it is only fitting that we get used to talking this outrageous baby talk to one another now.

Peculiarly good news

In the past fifty to one hundred years of U.S. Christianity, the true meaning of being a Christian has been lost to the vast majority of those calling themselves Evangelicals. There has been a slow, insidious paradigm shift toward a moralism that has nothing to do with true faith. We invite people into the faith and into our churches only to teach them how to act, what to do, what to think and how to look good (i.e. be a good witness). Their hearts, habits and core beliefs remain remarkably unchanged. The truth of this is borne out by the fact that the statistics for the Evangelical community reflect little difference from the secular community when comparing them in divorces, alcoholism, kids on drugs, pre-marital sex and a (fanatical) devotion to materialism. There is a disconnect somewhere. Our faith does not change us. This is because so much of what we have known as Christianity has little to do with faith. It has much more to do with works and giving the proper outward appearances.

The way to Life is simply this: believe in the Lord Jesus Christ and you will be saved. Again, most of us categorize this statement as an evangelistic or come-to-Jesus statement. To be certain it is. However, it is also the sum total of living life everyday as a Christian. Our beliefs will change us. We will begin to act and look like that thing or person into which we place our faith and trust. In a post-September 11 America, we have seen first-hand how people's beliefs can motivate them to radical action. The terrorists who killed themselves in the 9/11 attacks did not do so because someone kept telling them over and over again to do the "right thing." No, they did so because they were convinced in their heart of hearts, deep in their belief system, that this was the highest expression of devotion to their god. And on the opposite end of the spectrum, Mother Teresa did her work because she believed that when she touched the bodies of lepers, she was touching the body of Christ. Our beliefs change the way we live.

But I am getting ahead of myself. Let me briefly summarize the Gospel message and then I want you to hear the ecstatic praise of one who was totally bowled over by this message.

The Good News consists of two parts–"I've got good news and I got bad news... " First, the bad news. You and I are absolutely horrible. We were born sinful and everyday since we have added onto our skill as sinners. We are self-centered in every way. Even our good deeds drip with self-ishness and self-righteousness. We are God-haters and people-haters. We live for our own comfort, pleasures and independence from God. Some of us are better at keeping a lid on outward manifestations of this sickness but still we are all the same in our wickedness.

The good news is that God has decided to love folks like you and me. Even more than that, He wants us in His family. But there is a catch: to be in God's family we need to be perfect. That's a pretty big hurdle for folks like you and me. Actually, it is an impossible hurdle. This is where the good news really gets good. God knows that perfection is impossible for us, yet He still wants us in His family. So He provided a way for us to become perfect–with no effort our part–only faith is required.

The provision that God supplied for us is in Jesus Christ. Jesus came to live a perfect life for us. He then died to take the punishment that we deserve. Let me give you an example. Pretend you are on trial for embezzlement. You are guilty. The court also finds you guilty. You are sentenced to ten years in a state prison. But as the sentence is pronounced your father steps forward and speaks with the judge. The judge informs your father that the penalty must be carried out or else the law is a joke and has no meaning. Your father sighs. He takes a long look at you and then turns back to the judge and offers himself as the one to take the punishment; the one to spend the next ten years of his life in prison. The law will be satisfied. But know this, the judgement would be correct only if the father was not guilty. In other words, he had no debt to the law. If he did have a debt to the law his offer would be somewhat frivolous. The judge would have said, "Yes, I see here in your past several offenses which require you to serve time in prison. So forget about your son; you've got your own crimes to pay for." So you see, only an innocent party could take the punishment which another deserved.

This is what happened for us on the Cross. Jesus offered himself as the innocent substitute for you and me. God wanted to have us close to Himself. He wanted us in His family; therefore, he provided a way for this adoption to take place through the substitutionary atonement of Jesus. He took the punishment we deserve and we are free to live without serving out the punishment. So, in the Gospel, God comes to you and me and says that we can be a part of His family if we will only lay down our (drab, failing) attempts at life and cling to Jesus as the one who took the punishment in our place. (1 Cor. 5:21)

But wait… there is more. Jesus not only took our punishment; He also gave us His record. When Jesus took our record of sin and shame, He gave up His record of total righteousness and gave it to us. So we are not left with just a blank file–with no crimes attributed to us, but we have His record and His righteousness as our own. So when God the Father looks at us, He no longer sees our long list of sins and crimes, but He now sees the record of righteousness given to us by His Son. Amazing! Astounding! Almost beyond belief.

Now if this Gospel really begins to take hold of us, we are changed. We are filled with joy. We are utterly bowled-over. And in light of this "unbelievable" truth, let's take a look at what the Apostle Paul had to say when he started to unpack all this stuff and see the reality of it in his life. By the way, in the course of this book I will be quoting Scripture and, if you are like me when I am reading a book like this, you will briefly skim over it, look at the reference and say to yourself, "Yeah, yeah I know this… let's move on." Please don't be like me. Stop being so arrogant. Really, truly read the Scripture passage and ask God for the Spirit to teach more of His truth through this passage. For in the scheme of eternity, these passages will mean much more than anything I will say. That being said, let's look at the thoughts of a man crazy in love:

> *What can we say about such wonderful things as these? If God is for us, who can ever be against us? Since God did not spare even his own Son but gave him up for us all, won't God, who gave us Christ, also give us everything else? Who dares accuse us whom God has chosen for his own? Will God? No! He is the one who has given us right standing with himself. Who then will condemn us? Will Christ Jesus? No, for he is the one who died for us and was raised to life for us and is sitting at the place of highest honor next to God, pleading for us. Can anything ever separate us from Christ's love? Does it mean he no longer loves us if we have trouble or calamity, or are persecuted, or are hungry or cold or in danger or threatened with death? (Even the Scriptures say, "For your sake we are killed every day; we are being slaughtered like sheep.") No, despite all these things, overwhelming victory is ours through Christ, who loved us. And I am convinced that nothing can ever separate us from his love. Death can't, and life can't. The angels can't, and the demons can't. Our fears for today, our worries about tomorrow, and even the powers of hell can't keep God's love away. Whether we are high above the sky or in the deepest ocean, nothing in all creation will ever be able to separate us from the love of God that is revealed in Christ Jesus our Lord. (Romans 8:31-39, NLT)*

Do you hear it? Can you sense the wildness of a man set free– really free? Here is a fellow traveler so in love with the Gospel and its ramifications he can scarcely contain himself. The God of the Universe is pleading our case. He is deeply, truly in love with us. He is protecting us and standing with us so that, no matter what else happens, He will be there to love up on us.

OK, OK, I just took us to the fire hydrant again but there is a simple truth here that I am trying to teach my crazy heart. God loves me in Christ Jesus. That's it. That's what I know... some of the time. And that is beginning to be the comfort of my life. We have heard it over and over again. We have heard preachers say it. We have heard drunks shout it. We have heard enemies quote it and we ourselves have bandied it about (with little awareness of its meaning) for most of our lives: "God loves you." Saying it and typing it again, I am struck by the hollow ring this phrase has in my heart. It's just too common. Yet this is the goal, the desire and the ambition of my life and this book: to understand that God loves us.

In the coming chapters, I will attempt to sort out this bizarre mystery of God's grace as it shows itself in my life and heart. I invite you to come with me, walk with me, limp with me and discuss the immense implications of this "stupid" little phrase: God loves you!

Jesus loves me, loves me still, Though I'm very weak and ill... Yes, Jesus
loves me! Yes, Jesus loves me! Yes, Jesus loves me! The Bible tells me so.
~Anna B. Warner

Chapter Three

Pronouns:
The Most Critical Aspect
Of The Gospel!

Peculiar People does a show on Martin Luther, the
Protestant Reformer. In this show we quote Luther when he
exclaims the headline above. "Pronouns! The most critical
aspect of the Gospel!" He goes on to explain, "YOU; ME; the
Christ who gave Himself for US! Wrap your arms around it
and love such a Gospel!" And indeed it is true. If the Gospel
is not 100 percent applicable to pronouns, then it is no
Gospel (good news) at all. Yet there is one pronoun that
seems to be constantly lagging behind the others in the arena
of Faith, and it is the pronoun ME.

Do you find it easier to speak to others about God's great love for THEM but feel a slight (or great) disconnection when thinking or speaking about God's great love for you? Is there a nagging doubt in your heart concerning just how much you can rely on God's forgiveness? Do you find it difficult to run to the Father with abandonment—knowing what a "rotten kid" you have been in the past week?

We have a wonderful pastor friend, Rick Downs. He tells the story of counseling a college girl concerning her constant sense of shame and guilt in spite of knowing the Good News of the Gospel. She was constantly depressed and truly felt she was "good for nothing." She let out a barrage of invectives about herself. She said she was stupid, could do nothing right, was lazy, selfish, ugly, etc. When she finished, Rick asked her to bring to mind someone who was her close friend. Once the girl had the friend in mind Rick asked her what she would say to someone who had spewed the same indictments on her close friend as she had just done on herself. The girl was silent for a few minutes with her head bowed. She looked up with tears flowing and said, "I would say to that person, 'How dare you!! How dare you say such horrible things about my friend!'"

Some of us find it so much easier to give grace to others than to ourselves. The promises are true for others because, in our minds, others are so much better than we are. We know ourselves and our devious, horrible side, so we really don't deserve the promises the way Jane or John do.

Me: The most critical of the critical pronouns

While there is an overwhelming overemphasis on "ME" in our society, I want to focus our discussion today on the "ME" in regard to true faith and belief. First, we would do well to remember that our hearts, our minds, even our very souls are the territory of a vast spiritual war; a war that is beyond our ability to imagine or comprehend. We would be (or should I say WILL be) amazed at the conflict and battles that rage around us on a daily basis. Most of the things we consider freak accidents or frustrating circumstances are actually the results of a spiritual reality beyond our consciousness. Paul exhorts us to prayer because we DO NOT wrestle against flesh and blood, but against these spiritual realities.

Second, we should understand that our flesh stays in a constant state of rebellion toward the Gospel. The flesh always wants to measure our performance and our worthiness in comparison to others or in comparison to our own standards of "holiness." Satan uses this tendency of the flesh and stokes the fire with ample fuel to make our conscience burn with doubt and fear when we approach God. We often go to God with a fading hope that somehow He will love us in spite of our record of sins from the past week or so. But with the "help" of Satanic influence this fading hope turns into a practical denial of grace in our hearts.

The third thing to remember when considering grace for our own lives is our capacity to water-down most Biblical truth to the point of bland bits of trivia. This is especially true when we consider the truth for ourselves. We water-down the Good News because we feel guilty about being ecstatically happy about Jesus while knowing that our lives are such a mess. Therefore, we have learned to keep the excitement about grace well under control lest we seem hypocritical in our own eyes.

The fourth thing that keeps us from experiencing grace and the wonder thereof: our knowledge of ourselves!! We keep thinking that God couldn't really love us all that much, because He really knows the TRUTH about us, and so do we! So when we think about God's unconditional love, it has to be for other people who are not quite as "messed-up" as we are!

We're all rascals!!

Let me tell it to you plainly: all of us are so "messed-up" that if God ever gave us a vision of what we are like in our flesh, we would wilt and die! Isaiah got a little taste of this when he was transported to heaven. And he cried out, "Woe is me for I am a man of unclean lips!" Luther said that even our repentance (the most holy act of human beings) needs to be repented of! Everyday, no matter how "well" or how poorly you've lived for Christ, you need grace to have God accept you. YOU!! ME!! You are no different than I. We have absolutely impure motives and desires about the holiest things in our lives! How many times have you studied your Bible or had morning devotions only to use that information later in a conversation with others to prove what a "holy" person you are??? How many times have you risen from prayer believing that you are "perfect" in your heart and righteousness, only to find hate and resentment rising to the surface as you encounter co-workers or family members?

The point I am making here is just this: YOU ARE A HUGE, GREAT, BIG, OUTRAGEOUS SINNER and need grace whenever you go to God. And that is where the good news comes in… God loves huge, great, big, outrageous sinners! Stop thinking that this grace only applies to those who know how to "walk the walk." To be quite honest, most of those people "walking the walk" in the Evangelical community are so filled with brazen self-righteousness that their walk is really just a strut! Strutting their "holiness" so everyone else will feel inferior to them.

Brother, Sister, the Gospel applies to you. Did you hear me? It applies to YOU. It applies to ME or it is no Gospel at all. Stop holding back. Stop thinking that the Good News is just for other people who aren't as bad as you! The lesson of Matthew, Mark, Luke and John is this: Jesus came for sinners. Are you a sinner? Then rejoice because Jesus came and died for YOU. For ME. Love those pronouns!

What a Gospel. What a Friend. What a Savior!!

Chapter Four

The Rich Kid

Once upon a time there was a young boy, named Christopher Deo, who was very, very rich. Actually, the boy himself was not rich but his parents were, which by extension, made the young son wealthy as well. However, wealth and ease had not always been Chris' life. As a matter of fact, he was once quite a ruffian. Chris was born the child of a drug-addicted stripper and his father was thought to be a member of the Hell Raisers motorcycle gang. Chris' mother was so deep into her own problems and failure that she soon lost interest in the young boy. Really, it was a bit harsher than just losing interest. It was a cruel neglect and disgust for the young child of a Hell Raiser.

So it was no surprise when, at the age of six, Chris wandered off to become the youngest member of a gang of hoodlums who lived on the streets as adolescent renegades. One of the things that these gamins found particularly delightful was to go to the Deo mansion on the hill and throw stones at the windows. You see, they hated the Deo family. They despised their nice home, their orderly life and the abundant provisions of the rich. So the young hell raisers took great pleasure in wreaking havoc on rich people whenever they could. Actually, throwing stones was only one of the vandalistic activities these imps would perpetrate on the rich Deo household. They would spread the most horrible stories about them. Whenever the subject of the Deo family was raised, they would be there to tell deliberate lies about the Deos. Once they saw the Deo mini-van parked at the grocery store. Chris kept a lookout while the other hooligans let all the air out of the tires. They truly despised this family and every thought of them was fueled by a seething hatred that was not at all natural.

One particularly sticky summer night, the lazy young delinquents decided that it was time to go and break some windows in the Deo home. It was a bit strange, but for some reason, Chris was not as excited about this activity as he had been in the past. For several weeks now, he had been having uncharacteristically kind and sympathetic thoughts towards the Deo clan. He couldn't explain it, but when the opportunity came to pester them again, he wasn't very hip to the idea. But he went along anyway, afraid to show his reluctance.

Chris and the gang sneaked through the fence of the Deo mansion but they did not notice the new laser security system that had been installed around the perimeter. As each perpetrator jumped over the fence onto the Deo property, a silent alarm was triggered to call the police. The boys giggled, smirked and laughed as they gathered stones. They began looking for just the right window to break. A window that was not too easy; one that would be a challenge for one of the boys to hit with a rock. Just as they had settled on the "betcha can't hit that" window, they heard cars approaching. At first they were not worried but then they saw the whirling blue and red lights of the police cars. Panic ensued. The gang ran like a nest of cockroaches. Most ran for the fence, including Chris. But right as the young gangster reached the very top, he felt the strong grip of a law officer's hand on his ankle. The grip tightened and Chris was pulled down from the fence and into a waiting pair of handcuffs.

Once at the police station, Chris was fingerprinted and placed in a holding room. He tried to act like he wasn't scared, but he was. He tried to pretend that he was tough, but he wasn't. He tried not to cry and he didn't. But he sat in the small room with a steel door and thought about his life. He was too young to know the psychology or the ramifications of living life as an orphaned bastard child of a motorcycle gang member. All he knew was that as he looked at his life, he was impressed by what he didn't see. He didn't see family. He didn't see the love and fun that the kids on TV seemed to have. He didn't see a mother who cared and he didn't see a father who would teach and guide. Thinking like this had it's final result in tears and sorrow.

Just as the tears were falling from his bowed head onto the cement floor, Chris heard the door open. He quickly wiped the tears away. In walked a policeman who looked eight feet tall. Behind him was Mr. Deo!

The policeman sneered towards Chris and said, "Here he is Mr. Deo. He's the only one we caught, but from the looks of him, he was probably the worst of the lot anyway."

Chris had to smile, if only on the inside, at the policeman's stupidity. He wasn't the worst of the gang. He wished he were, but he was just the puppy of the pack and he wasn't nearly as tough as the others.

Mr. Deo spoke, "What will happen to him?"

The officer replied, "Can't find a proper address or guardian for him. We'll hold him here for a day or so. Take 'im to Juvenile Court and then on to detention."

That word "detention" made Chris' hair stand on end. The other boys had told stories about detention and what happened to them there. Jack still had a scar across his stomach where he had gotten into a fight with a real mean kid there.

Mr. Deo spoke again, "What if I don't press charges?"

"Mr. Deo, now don't take this the wrong way, but that would be very unwise. These kids have been pestering you and your family for years. It's about time we made an example of at least one of 'em," said the Officer.

"Yes, I understand. And that's just what I intend to do. I am going to make an example of this Chris Garner."

Chris was shocked to hear this name spoken by Mr. Deo. Garner was the last name of the Hell Raiser dad who had gotten his mother pregnant. Chris never used the last name Garner unless he was trying to look tough. He had given the police his mother's last name, Davis. But somehow Mr. Deo knew. And now Mr. Deo would make an example of him. But he wasn't going to press charges. Chris wondered if Mr. Deo would bribe the policeman to leave them alone in the room so Mr. Deo could beat him. Then maybe he would send him out to the streets again and the other fellas could see how badly he had been beaten. Or maybe Mr. Deo wasn't pressing charges and would wait for Chris to walk out of the police station where he would kidnap him and possibly kill him.

Mr. Deo looked down at Chris. He was even smiling! What kind of diabolical man was this? Smiling about killing a little kid.

Mr. Deo spoke, "Well, Chris, how would you like that? Would you like for me to make an example of you?"

"Do whatcha want," Chris said. "I'm not afraid of you anyway. And if you think I'm gonna beg you to be easy on me, you're dead wrong! I'm not scared of you."

"Well, that's good," said Deo, "because I don't want you to be scared of me. I want us to learn to like each other."

The policeman interrupted, "Mr. Deo, I can appreciate you trying to have pity on the kid, but you don't know this kind. This kind of trash will take whatever you got and then bite ya when you're not looking. They just aren't safe. Don't let your good nature get the better of you."

"Officer Denton, could we step outside and talk? I want to ask you some questions about my plan of action here," said Deo.

Chris thought to himself, "I was right. I knew I was right. He's bribing the cop and he's gonna take me somewhere to beat me. What a mean man; looking down at me and smiling and talking about learning to like each other. Let's face it, I'm a dead man."

Chris stayed in the room for a couple more hours. Suddenly the door was thrown open again. It scared Chris and he looked up to see the same two men. Denton said to Mr. Deo, "OK, Mr. Deo, he's all yours and good luck."

In the Grasp of Deo

Chris struggled as Mr. Deo began leading him out of the police station. In the end, Mr. Deo was actually dragging Chris as they approached the Deo family car. Chris was certain that his death (or near-death experience) was at hand. He tried as hard as he could to act unafraid. For awhile he said nothing as Mr. Deo drove the car into the night.

"What are you gonna do with me?" asked Chris.

"Well," said Deo, "since you have no record of address… no home to go to, I thought I would take you to my home. How does that sound?"

"What are you going to do me? I'm not scared of no beatin'. I can take anything you can dish out," Chris said, hoping to show enough bravado to make himself look hard and mean.

"Chris, this may be difficult for you to understand right now, but what I am going to do to you is for your own good. You won't believe it right away, but…"

"Oh, right! I've heard this one before," said Chris with an attitude. "This is going to hurt me more than it hurts you. No wonder they call you DeadHead Deo."

Mr. Deo laughed. He was laughing at Chris' statement but also he laughed at Chris' tough guy act. "Chris, this really might hurt you, but not the way you think. You see, I'm going to take you home and I am going to seek out the legal means to adopt you. I want to be your father."

This was too much to comprehend. Chris couldn't believe it. His heart wanted to leap at the news but Chris had learned that if something seems too good to be true it probably is. His learned reaction to bad news took over.

"Who said I need a father? And besides I know what you got planned. You're not wantin' a son, you want a slave! You think just because you caught me that I owe you or something. I'm not gonna work for you or any other..."

Just then the car turned into the drive at the Deo mansion. Suddenly the house looked different to Chris. He no longer saw it as a source of jealousy and envy, rather he was excited by the prospect of actually going inside. Maybe he could steal something to show the guys to prove that he had really been inside. He was a mass of conflicting emotions. Thoughts swirled around his head like a whirlwind.

"Could this possibly be true?"

"How can I escape?"

"Watch out, Deo is gonna trick you! Nothin' is this easy."

"What did he mean about adopting me?"

"I betcha he has a dungeon and he's going to take you there and chain you and torture you."

"What if he is telling the truth?"

"Where am I? Is this a sick dream?"

Chris' thoughts ran faster and further than I can ever tell you in a story. He was a maze of wonder and apprehension. The car pulled into a four-car garage. Standing in the doorway on the other end of the garage was a tall figure; a man in a tuxedo. Mr. Deo got out of the car. Chris stayed very still. Ever since they pulled into the drive, he had not spoken a word. He was afraid. He was afraid that this was a trick, a joke and he was afraid that it might be true.

"Here he is, Hollis. This is the new member of the family. Be sure and take good care of him," said Deo as he opened the door for Chris.

Hollis came over to the car, took a long look at Chris and smiled deeply. "He's really quite wonderful, isn't he, sir?"

Deo laughed again. "Yes, yes that's a good way of putting it. 'Quite wonderful.'"

Chris could feel his throat tighten and as much as he tried to stop it, tears formed in his eyes. No one had ever said that about him. As matter of fact, no adult had ever looked at him and smiled. He wanted to crack a snappy joke or act like he wasn't affected by this compassion, but he could only sit in the car seat while tears rolled down his cheeks.

Hollis and Deo led Chris into the mansion. The mansion was more than he could have imagined. More than he had ever seen. More than he had ever felt. He was taken to a room; his room. His room. That's what Mr. Deo said. The room was fixed-up to be the neatest kid's room ever. There were planes and rocket ship models hanging from the ceiling. The bedframe looked like a race car. The sheets were crispy clean and smelled like fragrant soap. "Quite wonderful." That's all he could think about. Quite wonderful. The house was quite wonderful. The room was quite wonderful. And someone had looked at him and spoken the words, "Quite wonderful." If there was a heaven, he thought, this must be it.

Mr. Deo and Hollis watched Chris as he wandered with amazement through his new room. They were filled with joy as Chris found each new wonder. They were warmed with delight to be able to provide for the little orphan. Much more was ahead, but for now they were enjoying the awe-inspiring moment.

Mr. Deo dismissed Hollis and walked over to the bed where Chris was sitting and bouncing, testing out the new mattress. Mr. Deo pulled up a chair. Chris looked down into his lap, not knowing how to respond or what to say. Not knowing if any of this was real or some cruel joke to punish him.

"Well, Chris Garner," said Deo.

There it was again! Deo had used his father's last name; the name of the gang member. The name that had always helped Chris pretend that he was tough. Mr. Deo noticed his surprise.

"Yes, Chris. I know who your father was. I know much more about you than you could ever understand. I know of your mother and I know about how hard life has been for you. I also know all the bad things you have done and how much you have hated me in the past."

Chris started to say something but he couldn't find the words. Deo knew everything. Chris couldn't even think of a good lie or some other excuse for himself. He did exactly what he did not want to do; he cried.

Mr. Deo rose from his chair, sat on the bed next to Chris and then he did something that Chris could never remember ever happening. Mr. Deo picked him up, cradled him like a baby and held him close to his chest.

At first, Chris fought and tried to get away but then at last he gave in to the warmth and comfort of Deo. Chris cried and cried. The dam had broken and all the fears, heartaches and puzzles of his young life came gushing out in torrents of tears. The warmth of Mr. Deo's body and the smell of his spice after-shave made Chris drunk with love. Love. He had never really known this emotion before. He knew it was missing but did not really know what it felt like.

Mr. Deo rocked gently back and forth while Chris cried. Then Mr. Deo cried. Mr. Deo's tears rolled down his cheek onto Chris, baptizing the young boy's head. Together they were a "perfect mess" of love and sorrow.

Finally, Mr. Deo spoke softly, "Oh, Chris. Dear Chris. What a tender heart you have and how diligently you have tried to hide it. And what a wonderful thing life is but I see how all the forces of evil have tried to keep you from experiencing the wonder."

Chris began sobbing as he looked up to see Mr. Deo's tears. No one had ever cried for him before. No one.

"Chris, you're home now. I plan to adopt you and make you my own. And I want to give you all the things that you have missed until now. I want to lavish you with wonderful things. I will be so proud to call you my son. It may not make sense to you now but Chris I want you to know that I love you. I really love you."

Chris nearly fainted. All he could do was lay there in Deo's arms and listen. Then Mr. Deo said some more things that washed over Chris like spring rain. He felt clean. He felt hopeful. He felt, possibly for the first time in a decade. And the feeling he had was love. Mr. Deo finally said good night with the promise of more tomorrow.

Chris lay wide-eyed and fast awake beneath the clean sheets trying to understand what had happened to him. After several hours, Chris slept the sleep of rest. True rest. And for the first time his small frame relaxed, shedding the anxiety of the ages.

Chapter Five

Chris Finds A Home

Chris woke the next morning filled with many emotions on each end of the spectrum! He could not believe what had happened to him. He was overwhelmed with the love of Deo but he could not believe completely that things were really all that simple. What if Mr. Deo woke up this morning and came to his senses? He might come barging through the bedroom door with all the rage and anger of... of... well, of most normal people who had been so badly treated by a young boy. What if all this had been some cruel joke and today would be the day that Deo or Hollis would come and beat him? Yeah, what if they beat him and then make him their slave?

"That's it!" he thought to himself. "Of course, that would be the best revenge! To sucker me in on all this love and compassion then turn and kick me in the stomach. What a idiot I was! Deo is much more devious than I thought."

He was sitting on the side of his bed looking out on the manicured lawn of the estate, thinking and fearing, when there was a knock on the door after which Hollis came in carrying some new clothes. Chris recoiled at Hollis' entrance but then settled down to listen to him.

"Here are some fresh clothes for you," said Hollis. "After breakfast, perhaps we can go together to pick out more. I hope I have divined the correct size."

Chris looked at the new clothes. He could not remember ever having brand new clothes before. And he certainly couldn't imagine what it would be like to go and pick out clothes at a store! But was he being tricked? Was all this real?

"These clothes will be great… I mean, they'll be alright," said Chris, trying not to look too excited. "So what's the scoop here? Is all this real? What do I have to do? When do I get my punishment? Where's the catch?"

"My dear boy, I assure you 'this' is all real! Mr. Deo has had his eye on you for quite some time," Hollis said as he laid the clothes beside Chris. "I suggest you take a shower and get dressed. This will be a busy day."

"What about Mr. Deo? What do you mean, 'He has had his eye on me?'"

"All in good time, my boy. All in good time," said Hollis as he left the room with a wink.

Chris held the new clothes to his face and smelled the freshness. He hugged himself and he hugged life for the first time.

"This really might be true," he thought to himself as he headed for the shower.

The story continues...
but not here

The stories and tales of Chris' adoption and his finding a place of belonging in this world could string on and on. And perhaps one day I shall tell them all to you, but, in your heart, you know most of the stories already. They are stories very similar to yours. But that too, is for another time. I would like to end this narrative with a story of the day that Chris was re-united with his old gang.

One wonderful spring day Chris was on an errand for his new father. He was walking downtown. It was not a surprise to run into his gang; he knew where they hung out. But it was quite a shock for young Chris to see how different they looked now. He had never before noticed the dirt and smudges on their faces. The clothes, which were more like rags, hung from their skinny bodies like they were hanging from a clothesline.

The gang surrounded Chris. It appeared that they were as shocked as Chris when they noticed his appearance. Both parties ogled one another for a few moments. Finally Rifle spoke,

"Hey Chris, is that you? What happened?"

"I've been adopted by Mr. Deo!" said Chris with just a hint of fear. His fear was well justified. After a moment of disbelief, the boys began to mock him and tease him.

"Ohhh, adopted by MR. DEO!!! ADOPTED BY MR. DEO."

"Daaaay- OOO. I said, Daaay-OOO."

The boys were dancing around Chris. Then began the shoving and the hitting.

"Stop it!! Cut it out, guys!!" cried Chris. "Listen, it's true. I don't know why and I'm still not sure what his plans for me are, but we had him all wrong! Mr. Deo is a wonderful man. Really. As a matter of fact, he said that if I ever see you guys again I should tell you that he will adopt you too! Honest."

Buster Butt hit Chris across the mouth. "Why would we want to be adopted by that old crazy? You don't think we're good enough just like we are? We don't need no adoption to make us 'good people.' What's wrong with you, man? Look at you. You look like a fag, all dressed up like that. So now tell us, what has Deo got you doing? How are you paying for your 'adoption?'"

"No, guys. You got the wrong idea. I don't have to do anything. Mr. Deo loves me. He really does. Sure, I got chores and there are plenty of things that keep me busy. I'm going to school now and I study real hard. But I don't have to do it to make him love me. He loved me first. He cried with me. He has given me so much, I would work for him forever."

Finally Randy, spoke. "OK, Shrimp. Let's get this straight. You raise hell all your life. You get caught breaking windows on Deo's mansion. He takes you home and adopts you. Is that what you are trying to tell me?"

"Well, yeah," said Chris. "I know it sounds weird but it's true. He told me he loves me and he shows it every day."

Randy continued his questioning. "So do you get 'loved' when you go out and raise hell? What about now. What if you went out and raised some hell with us tonight? You think Deo would still love you?"

"I think so," stammered Chris. "No, I know so. He would still love me."

"Well, Chris, old buddy, if you get all this 'love' and if Deo showers you with presents when you're a hell raiser, why don't we go out and raise more hell than ever before? Cause it seems like the more stinking bad you are, the more Deo is going to love you. Let's break all the windows in his house!! I'll bet he'll REALLY love us then."

All the boys laughed. Chris searched for an answer. Finally, he spoke from his heart.

"Look, it's hard to explain. But you don't understand. My life is not about what I do and what I don't do. My life goes deeper than that now. Yeah, I could break windows, get drunk and fart around with you guys all night and Mr. Deo would still love me. But I'm not a hell raiser anymore. I am a member of a new family and I have a new identity. So… yeah, Mr. Deo loves me so much that I could be real bad with you and the more gross my life, the more he would love me. But my heart is no longer there… or here with you guys. My heart is with Mr. Deo."

"Well then, should we keep on sinning so that God can show us more and more kindness and forgiveness? Of course not! Since we have died to sin, how can we continue to live in it? Or have you forgotten that when we became Christians and were baptized to become one with Christ Jesus, we died with him? For we died and were buried with Christ by baptism. And just as Christ was raised from the dead by the glorious power of the Father, now we also may live new lives. Since we have been united with him in his death, we will also be raised as he was. Our old sinful selves were crucified with Christ so that sin might lose its power in our lives. We are no longer slaves to sin." (Romans 6:1-6, NLT)

Moralism...can ultimately only create awareness of sin and guilt or manufac-
tured virtues built on will power. A ministry which leads to genuine sanctification
and growth, on the other hand, avoids moralism, first by making clear the deep
rootage of sin-problems in the flesh so that the congregation is not battling these
in the dark, and then by showing that every victory over the flesh is won by faith
in Christ, laying hold of union with Him in death and resurrection and relying on
His Spirit for the power over sin.... Ministries which attack only the surface of
sin and fail to ground spiritual growth in the believer's union with Christ produce
either self-righteousness or despair, and both of these conditions are inimical to
spiritual life. ~Richard Lovelace.

Chapter Six

God's Favor And
Daily Devotions

If you're a member of the Evangelical subculture (conservative brand of Baptist, Presbyterian, Methodist, Bible Church, etc.) then you are well aware of that sacrosanct ritual called the Quiet Time (QT) or Daily Devotions (DD). I will be spending a great deal of time talking about this ritual. I believe that for many Christians it has become one of the primary stumbling blocks to exercising true faith.

Most of us have heard numerous talks, sermons and bits of advice on the importance of having a daily QT. So for many of us, the QT has become the lifeline that both establishes and maintains our Christian life.

As we get to know one another in these pages, you will, no doubt, encounter one or more of our four dogs. We cannot have children, so raising our dogs is as close as we get to parenting and/or observing another creature live with us. In order of appearance our dogs are: Mocha, the oldest and muttiest of our three canines; Bear, a Chocolate Lab and Golden Retriever mix; Java, our Rottwieler; and finally, Latté, a German Shepherd/Husky mix. I won't take time now to go into the various personality traits and quirks peculiar to each dog. You'll be getting that soon enough. But I do want to tell you about my dogs and their Daily Devotions. And you didn't think dogs had devotions did you??

Our dogs are, for the most part, house dogs. They are well-disciplined and have learned certain routines and habits that make life together more enjoyable. One of the routines we have established is that the dogs sleep in the bonus room and they don't come out until they are given permission in the morning. This makes for some rather jolly fun each morning as I rise and go into the bathroom to collect my robe and slippers. They hear me preparing to come and get them, then the time of devotion starts. Mocha and Bear begin to inch their way across the threshold of the bonus room, literally squirming with delight that it is another wonderful day and that their master is coming to greet them. The closer I get, the more excited they become. I usually stop at this point and tell them to get back across the threshold because I haven't "given the word" yet. They can hardly contain themselves. Joyously reluctant they wiggle back across the threshold and wait for me to enter the room. When I do, I reach down and begin to stoke them as I say, "Good Morning! Good Morning! How are my dogs this morning? Good Morning!" Well, this just sends them over the edge! They begin whining, wagging, jumping, smiling, laughing all because they know they are loved by their master and they can't wait to show their love in return. If this is getting a little icky for you, be patient.

It's not a religion...
It's a relationship

In our Evangelical circles we have heard this phrase over and over again, "It's not a religion, it's a relationship!" Or perhaps you have endeavored to interest others in Christianity by using this one: "How would you like to have a personal relationship with Jesus Christ?" Pretty heavy stuff, eh? And 99 percent of us would say that we DO have a personal relationship with Jesus Christ, but I am wondering if our actions, thoughts and behaviors don't betray this core belief. You see, my dogs have a relationship with me and a huge part of that relationship is based upon their trust in my love toward them. Yet how do WE act? What are our true innermost thoughts when we are alone with God in the morning? Are we wriggling with excitement in the knowledge that He loves us more than we can possibly imagine. Does His love send us over the edge? Most times–NO! Why? Well, it's because so often we go to meet God with a mental check list of all the things we have done or didn't do to merit His love. We are hesitant at best.

Have you ever known someone close to you who was a down-and-dirty, God-hating sinner who suddenly trusted in Christ and his or her life was turned upside down? People like this are so outrageously joyful and happy in the faith. It's down right embarrassing, not to mention convicting. Well, what is going on there? How can they have so much joy? Most of us just sort of smirk to ourselves and think, "This won't last! It won't be long before they settle into a 'normal' Christian life." And don't get me started on what we mean by the "normal Christian life." Anyway, why are these people so overwhelmed by God and His Gospel? They are delirious in mirth because they understand that they have done NOTHING to commend themselves to God. NOTHING. Yet God loves them anyway! They look back on last month and see that they were out doing drugs, or screwing around, or getting drunk, or abusing themselves or others in some way; they have a horrible record! By all accounts, no one, especially the God of the universe should love them, BUT HE DOES!!! Shazam!! They run to God, trusting His love and basking in a new forgiveness they have never known.

Now contrast that with our typical approach to God after we have lived in the faith long enough to have built up a record of sorts. We go to God but before we do we look back on last month or last week or yesterday. It is then that we see that we almost measured up but not really. We begin to examine our "goodness" looking for some good deeds that will make feel us better about approaching God. If we find some things, then we approach God with a bit of arrogant aloofness knowing and showing that we really aren't that bad after all. OR perhaps we scour our record and find little or nothing to commend ourselves to God so we either shrink back and do a "safe" little Bible reading or we bag the whole thing altogether and decide that we will pray another time. Any of this pushing your hot buttons?

You see, my dogs (and that new believer we just talked about) have taught me how to have devotions. My dogs run to me in the morning totally trusting that I am gonna enfold them in my love. They have no doubts whatsoever. This trust and this happiness with which they approach me is one of the most joyful routines of my day. Now don't get me wrong, these dogs have a lot of things they could feel ashamed about; three-foot holes in the backyard, candy that is pilfered with candy wrappers littering the carpet. "Let's take the tissue out of the bathroom wastebaskets and spread on the floor" is one of their favorite games. Flowers are destroyed in pursuit of the sneaky mole or rabbit, dog hair and shedding EVERYWHERE. Plus they have bad breath, gas and B.O. I mean, they ARE dogs, ya know. But you know what? It would break my heart if these dogs would slink into a corner when I came into the room because they started thinking about how disappointed I must be in them. Soooooo… how about you? Do you greet God in the morning with the euphoria of a mad lover or even a happy dog? Or do you go to Him with your tail between your legs, doing your duty by having morning devotions so He won't be madder at you than He already is? Or worse yet, do you go to Him feeling pretty spiffy about yourself and how fortunate God is to have you on His team. Gag me with a spoon!

Whatever your past relationship with God has been, I dare you to start acting like a dog! I encourage you to make Him roar with laughter as He sees you running to him with joy. This is THE best devotional you will ever have. I promise.

(If you are trying to be like Christ)...you are no longer thinking simply about right or wrong; you are trying to catch the good infection from a Person. It is more like painting a portrait than like obeying a set of rules. And the odd thing is that while in one way it is much harder than keeping the rules, in another way it is far easier. Because, The real Son of God is at your side. He is beginning to turn you into the same kind of thing as Himself. He is beginning, so to speak, to "inject" His kind of life and thought, His love into you; beginning to turn the old man into a live man. The part of you that does not like it is the part that is still old. ~C.S. Lewis.

Chapter Seven

A Daily Devotional A Day Keeps The Doctor Away

Continuing my discussion of our attitudes toward daily devotions, I would like to posit a thought for consideration: for some of us, a Daily Devotional (DD) a day keeps the Doctor (the Great Physician, Jesus) away! Pretty radical statement, eh? Let me explain. Our radical friend, Steve Brown has said that theology and the love of theology can be one of the strongest, surest walls erected to keep God out of our hearts. Because you see, if we can substitute love FOR God with a love of ideas ABOUT God then many times we can fool ourselves into thinking they are one in the same. In actuality the eventual outcome is a burning love of our ideas about God!! Our flesh, our hearts are constantly looking for ways to avoid the Almighty; it's just part of the curse. However, as Christians, we know that avoiding God is not good. Therefore, what do we do? We go to God in our morning devotionals which, in the beginning, is a wonderful thing. We have devotions because want to worship God and draw close to Him. But our greasy, grimy flesh keeps looking for a way to run. Therefore, after months, or weeks, or even days, we start a subtle shift from having DD in order to love God to an insidious superstition of wanting to prove to ourselves and to God that we do love Him. Can you see the difference? One is a joyful embrace, the other is a checklist of goodness.

Let me bring the dogs into this again (see above). What if my dogs, who run to me each morning with absolute joy, suddenly became self-conscious about this whole bit. Rather than running, wiggling and wagging right away they started thinking, "You know, I am not really sure I am being the best dog I can be. I mean every morning I run to the master with the same old stuff. I wiggle and wag but am I really wagging in the best way? I lick his hands and face, but perhaps I should buy a book on licking and see how to really do it right. Besides, the master probably doesn't even want my licks after what a bad dog I've been. That hole I dug in the backyard… my pal Spot told me that several children and a couple of SUV's were lost down that hole last week. Yikes! Yeah, the master is probably pretty disappointed in me. But I still need to greet Him in the mornings. If I don't, he will be even madder at me. I know what I'll do. I'll book myself into one of those weekend seminars on Tail Wagging and I'll buy that set of tapes on "Licking With Purpose" by Dr. Dachshund. And in the meantime, I will show up to greet the master but I'll buy a neat devotional book that will give me just the right barks and whines to mutter, so I don't screw things up so badly. After all, I don't want to make him even more disappointed in me." So the dogs become so method-conscious about their devotions that much of the joy and spirit is whacked out of the whole process.

But then something really strange begins to happen. The dogs begin greeting me in the mornings with their books in tow, reading doggie thoughts about the master and they begin barking the most outlandish barks. The euphoria they once had is replaced by a concentrated, grunting effort to get things "right." In the meantime, the master (me) is feeling more and more left out of this process altogether. The joyful morning habit has become a chore and I am feeling more and more like a burden to the dogs than a friend. And then they begin to say to themselves, "Hey, I've greeted the master every single morning for the past three months! My greetings are actually getting to be pretty good. I think the master has to be impressed by how well I am doing this now. Yes, that old master is really beginning to see what a great dog I am. I've even stopped digging in the yard so much. And when I do dig, the holes aren't nearly as deep as before. Just look at all the wonderful things my devotionals have accomplished. If any of the other dogs ask me how to be a better dog, I'm gonna tell them, 'Just start doing your doggie devotionals. Do them right and you will see what a difference they will make. Doggie devotionals saved my relationship with my master!'"

Do you see how that dastardly, demented, doggie flesh turned a thing of joy into a thing of duty and drabness? Do you see how the cursed, crazed canine turned from loving the master to loving his love of the master? Do you see how the pitiful, petulant pup began to alienate the master with the "good" intention of loving him more?

What is our response? Go and do likewise? No, because we know that we already have. Oh dear me! We are dogs! No, we are worse than dogs because such a scenario as outlined above would never cross the heart of a dog! Oh no, here I am a Christian, yet I see that I have done nothing of any value to commend myself to the Master. I have really screwed things up! I am such a sinner!!!!

> *I have come to call sinners to turn from their sins, not to spend my time with those who think they are already good enough. (Luke 5:32 NLT)*

> *I greet the dogs in the morning, not canines who think they are better than dogs. (2 Charlie 6:20)*

Did the Law ever love me? Did the Law ever sacrifice itself for me? Did the Law ever die for me? On the contrary, it accuses me, it frightens me, it drives me crazy. Somebody else saved me from the Law, from sin and death unto eternal life. That Somebody is the Son of God (Who loved me and gave Himself for me). Hence, Christ is no Moses, no tyrant, no lawgiver, but the Giver of grace, the Savior, full of mercy…Visualize Christ in these His true colors. I do not say that it is easy. Even in the present diffusion of the Gospel light, I have much trouble to see Christ as Paul portrays Him. So deeply has the diseased opinion that Christ is a lawgiver sunk into my bones. ~Martin Luther

Chapter Eight

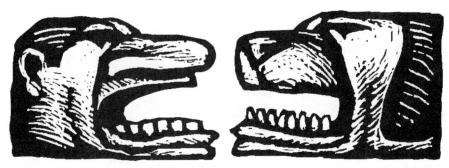

The Dastardly Devotional Duty

We are still talking about the danger of DD (Daily Devotionals). Of course, it is really "the thing" that DD have become (in our minds and hearts) which is the real danger. Suffice it to say that many of us Evangelicals have a tendency to turn anything of goodness and grace into law and duty. And as we come face to face with a law, we automatically think about the consequences of not obeying that law. In this matter we convince ourselves that the QT (Quiet Time) is a law that must be followed in order for us to be close to God. The consequence of not keeping this law? God's displeasure and His withdrawal from our lives. Once again let me remind you that this is not necessarily something that we would articulate to anyone but rather this is the subtle or vague feeling that begins to occupy our hearts. Therefore, the morning devotional becomes a barometer by which we measure our spirituality. Or even more horrifyingly, it becomes the measure of how much God will love us or be with us throughout the day. So what happens? DD becomes a law and the Bible says that the flesh (our human nature) will always try to break a law. (Just try NOT touching a freshly painted wall which has a sign on it declaring, "Wet Paint – Do Not Touch.") So here's the dilemma: we need DD because it makes us feel good, yet everything about our flesh rebels against having it.

Do it anyway?

So what's wrong? Why do we avoid DD? Well, there are a variety of reasons but let's just pick one for now. One reason we avoid our devotional time: it has become "dry" and boring. Now the traditional Evangelical answer to this dilemma is Do It Anyway!! Don't feel like it? Tough, do it anyway. Hate your neighbor? Tough, act like you love him anyway. Hate praying? Tough, pray anyway. In this prescription to our illness we uncover a death plot that begins to grow in our hearts. Inherent in the prescription to "do it anyway" is the belief that "doing" is sufficient even when the heart is not in line with love and grace. It is this "doing it anyway" that has fostered the fake Evangelical personality so prevalent in churches today. This Evangelical personality uses the aura of saccharin sweetness to clumsily hide a mass of anger, doubt and fear. It is this Evangelical personality that non-Christians see and steer away from.

But back to my point. The Scriptures tell us over and over again that God is after the heart. He is not as concerned with our actions as He is with the motive and intent of our actions (Ps. 51:16). The Pharisees are the ultimate example.

These are people who specialized in "doing it anyway." They did the right things at the right times with the right laws in front of the right people. Yet what does Jesus say about them? He said they were like a stinky coffin that had been painted nice and white. It looked pretty on the outside but inside was stench, corruption and corrosion (Matt. 23:27). How do you think the Pharisees got in this shape to deserve such a rebuke from Jesus? You guessed it: when confronted with the Law of God and realizing their heart's hatred of it, they ignored their hearts and "did it anyway."

So what am I advocating here? What is my prescription? My prescription is to listen to your heart. Or rather start being aware of your heart's deceitful, quirky nature. If you hate morning devotions the answer is not doing it anyway. The answer is to quickly find out why your heart is in such a state! Have you lost your "first love" for Christ? The answer is not to fake it and act like you still love Him with the excitement you once did. The answer is to look at the ingratitude and selfishness that have caused Him to be lowered in your eyes and heart. If the answer were to "do it anyway" then the Pharisees would have been praised by Jesus!!

However, in our Evangelical circles we have become so adept at doing, showing, attempting and faking our love for God that some of us begin to believe that the fakery is actually the "real McCoy." Thus we live defeated, sad lives on the inside while on the outside we "keep up our witness." But again I digress from my main point of DD. Why am I so pissed-off about morning devotions? The reason is simple. DD has become the graveyard for faith in many hearts. We use our DD as the ticket to God's love and compassion. We have DD not because we are head-over-heels in love with Christ but rather we fear His displeasure if we don't. We have DD because when we have kept up the habit for months, weeks or days we begin to feel pretty darn good about our goodness and our spirituality. We have DD because we want to make sure that God will go with us throughout the day. We have DD so we can drop some really spiritual conversations on our fellow believers. And before long we have convinced our hearts that all of the above reasons justify "Do It Anyway!" No wonder self-righteousness is such a problem in our churches.

I will be exploring the Biblical alternative to "doing it anyway" over the next several chapters. Stick around; it will be fun. Just remember that, more than anything else, God loves you in Christ Jesus far beyond your ability to understand or grasp.

Till men have faith in Christ, their best services are but glorious sins.
~Thomas Brooks

Chapter Nine

The Fix Is In... Or Has Been For Years

For the past several chapters I have been addressing the issue of the Danger of Daily Devotionals (DD). So now I would like to offer an alternative that, hopefully, will help us to approach God with joy and not duty. Are you ready? Get out your pencil and paper. Get ready to write this down. This is really THE ANSWER! OK, here goes! Drum roll please!... The solution is: FAITH!! That's right. Just good ol' down home, old-fashioned faith.

I can almost hear many of you groan. "Big deal! I know faith is an important part of my life in Christ, but what I really need is some profound twist of logic and truth that will help me in the nitty-gritty. Yeah, yeah right... faith."

Someone once approached Martin Luther and scolded him about the very same issue. They said that his preaching on faith alone was the lazy man's dream of religion. Belief alone was too easy and could not be taken seriously. To this charge Luther whipped around on his heels, pointed at his accuser and said, "Try it for just one hour!"

For just one hour live your life with no fear or worry, leaning solely on Christ alone. For just one hour believe that God is in total control of your life therefore you have no need to fret about your food, income or security. Give up all control of any situation, knowing that God will work things out for His glory. For just one hour let faith take you to the Throne Room of Heaven and catch a glimpse of the God of all Gods who loves you more than you love your own children. For just one hour have your life so focused on Christ that all other things look like garbage compared to His glory. All this requires faith and faith alone.

The downward spiral from faith to fear

For many of us, the concept of faith, or rather the act of faith, loses ground as we "grow" in the Christian life. Our minds become consumed with the "ought to's" and "better not's" of what we think Christianity is. We came to Christ by trusting in Him by faith but we soon lose sight of this trust as we "mature." Our love is quickly turned to duty as we are swept away into an anal-retentive sub-culture called Evangelicalism.

> SideBar: I come down hard on Evangelicals because I am one. I am conservative in my theology and take the Bible very seriously. The sins, excesses and foibles which I see in our subculture, I see only because I have the same proclivities.

There are "concerned brothers" out there who are more than happy to "share" with us their ideas on how we should behave, what we should do, what we should read, how we should react, and the type of "Christian" personality we should exhibit. Before long our hearts are drawn aside into a quagmire of fear and fakery. Jesus becomes a judge, not an advocate. God becomes a tyrant not a father. And one day we find that we have been Christians for many years yet we are uptight, nervous, pent-up, doubtful, fearful and suspicious. We lightly entertain the thought that maybe this Christianity thing was not really the right choice after all and perhaps we have wasted a good portion of our lives. But no! This can't be true. So we gird our loins and promise ourselves (and God) that we will be better, do better and try harder. Then we will have joy and freedom. We draw up new plans for discipline, prayer and Bible study and/or Daily Devotions! We then move out with our faces set like flint against the storms of fear and doubt.

This new determination becomes our measuring stick for how well we are doing "in the faith." Yet faith has NOTHING to do with such a plan! Can we not see that any unbeliever does the same thing? Every human being sees areas that have eluded his or her hopes and expectations and most everyone makes this same type of New Year's resolution to be better; all done without faith in Christ. So what makes our resolutions any different? As you look at your life and determine to be better, isn't Christ missing in the equation? In other words, are we made better by doing the "right" things or are we made better by uniting with Christ by faith? The apostle Paul asks the very same question of the Galatians. The Galatian Christians were folks who believed that, yes, faith in Christ saved you but growth in Christ only came through doing the right things. I'll let Paul speak for himself here:

> *"Oh, foolish Galatians! What magician has cast an evil spell on you? For you used to see the meaning of Jesus Christ's death as clearly as though I had shown you a signboard with a picture of Christ dying on the cross. Let me ask you this one question: Did you receive the Holy Spirit by keeping the law? Of course not, for*

the Holy Spirit came upon you only after you believed the message you heard about Christ. Have you lost your senses? After starting your Christian lives in the Spirit, why are you now trying to become perfect by your own human effort? You have suffered so much for the Good News. Surely it was not in vain, was it? Are you now going to just throw it all away? I ask you again, does God give you the Holy Spirit and work miracles among you because you obey the law of Moses? Of course not! It is because you believe the message you heard about Christ." (Galatians 3:1-5, NLT)

Read this carefully. Paul is, in essence, asking these people, "Does God give you His spirit and work miracles among you because you've gotten your act together and are doing the right things or is it because you believe what you heard?" The answer is obvious! It is because of their faith not their works.

So am I saying to "bag" your devotionals; stop having them? Yes, if you are in the least bit confused about your motives and intentions. What should you do instead? Believe. Believe again that God loves you in Christ Jesus more than you can ever imagine. Believe that it is not your part of a celestial bargain to do the right things so that God will do the right things toward you. Believe that Jesus loves you and is closer to you (in love) than any brother or family member. Believe that, when Christ paid for your sins, He really did pay for your sins and you can run to Him with all the joy of a child running toward his Daddy. Believe that God is for you 100 percent, all the time–100 percent of the time. Believe that God is smiling, laughing and dancing over you with joy. This is not the lazy man's approach to religion. This is a daring, active grasping onto the very core of life. Faith is far superior to religious deeds.

And if you affirm just one of these truths consistently throughout the day this will be far better than any morning devotional ever could be. Have faith.

I close this chapter with a quote by C.S. Lewis:

The main thing we learn from a serious attempt to practice the Christian virtues **is that we fail.**

If there was any idea that God had set us a sort of exam and that we might get good marks by deserving them, that has to be wiped out.

If there was any idea of a sort of bargain–**any idea that we could perform our side of the contract and thus put God in our debts so that it was up to Him to perform His side**–that has to be wiped out... every one has the idea of an exam or of a bargain; the first result of real Christianity is to blow that to bits.

– C.S. Lewis (emphasis mine)

Chapter Ten

"Do It Anyway" & The Death Of Faith

As I promised several pages ago, I now want to give you an illustration of how our prescriptions to love God more through the duty of DD (Daily Devotionals) actually exposes what lousy lovers we are. Let me set the stage once again. As we "grow" in the faith, many of us lose our joy and our first love for Christ. DD become dry rituals and we are tempted to "bag" it. Our normal Evangelical prescription for such a scenario is: DO IT ANYWAY. We have this sense that DOING something is sufficient and far better than not doing it. That is because as Westerners we are very oriented to results and outcome. This has taken hold in our Christianity.

I love you because...
well, uh... because I have to.

Now let me tell you a story about a married couple. Let's pretend it is Valentines Day in the home of Mr. and Mrs. EeeVan. Mr. E has been sort of moping around the house for several months. He is not really connecting with his wife. He has lost his "first love" for her. This concerns him but he has been told that if he just does the right things, he will be OK. On the day before Valentines Day he goes to buy a card and some chocolates for Mrs. E. As he reads through the various cards he remembers the day when indeed his love soared as depicted in the cards. He is saddened at his current state of affairs. He finds a card that says just enough but not too much because he doesn't want to seem too hypocritical. He signs the card and seals the envelope with a tiredness he has grown accustomed to in the past several months. On Valentines Day he rises, showers, shaves and goes to the breakfast table. His wife also awakens to have a cup of coffee with her hubby before he leaves for work. As she sits down, Mr. E hands her the card and the chocolates. He mumbles the words "love you" and drinks his coffee. Mrs. E is somewhat surprised and taken aback by this gesture. Mr. E has been so distant and pre-occupied she really didn't expect anything. But she tentatively takes the card and gift while trying to smile. Mr. E leaves for work feeling quite good about himself because he has done his duty. He considers himself to be "quite the husband" and an extraordinary man to do such loving things in spite of his true feelings.

Later in the day, Mrs. E re-reads the somewhat generic Valentines card. She misses the love they once had and wonders what is happening in their relationship. She calls Mr. E at work and confronts him.

"Honey, thank you for the card and candy but I feel that there is something wrong between us. Will you tell me what it is?"

Mr. E is somewhat shocked that perhaps Mrs. E hasn't fallen for his "do it anyway" maneuver. He decides to fess up.

"Wife, to be quite honest, I don't love you like I once did but (lucky for you) I have decided to do the right things and say the right things and ACT like I am in love with you even though we are really quite distant. Therefore, the card and chocolates I gave you this morning are further proof that, indeed, I am a very good husband and will continue to be so in the coming months."

Mrs. E, stunned to silence, hangs up the phone without a response. She cannot determine if she is more sad than angry or vice versa. She is sad that indeed their relationship has come to such a mechanical, antiseptic end. But she is angry that her husband would think that his actions alone are sufficient for any relationship!! Not only is he ignoring her and NOT loving her, but he is even feeling good about himself in the process!!! What a rat fink!

Doin' ain't feelin'

Does any of this sound familiar? What would you say to Mr. EeeVan? Would you say, "Hey keep up the good work. You are doing the right things. All that remains is the emotions and they will come if you keep it up?" Or perhaps you would say, "Stop! Stop this self-righteous, hypocritical approach to your wife! Go to her. Gaze into her eyes. Communicate deeply with her. Consider, reflect and repent about what a bad husband you have been, that you have allowed such a wonderful woman to drift from your heart. List again in your heart and mind those wonderful qualities that attracted you to her. Observe and appreciate all that she is and all that she has done for you and your home. Think back to the time when her smile made you twinkle inside. Meditate on the wonder of sharing your life with another human being. Understand that all your actions are for nothing if you don't have the love and emotions behind them. A monkey can do the right things but only a human being can feel deeply and communicate those feelings with his actions."

Well, you get the idea. I hope this little analogy will make you think about the horrible trap of "doing it anyway." I pray that we (together) will go once again and gaze into our Lover's eyes. That we will consider all those things we told Mr. E above and fall deeply in love with Jesus once again.

> *As Jesus and the disciples continued on their way to Jerusalem, they came to a village where a woman named Martha welcomed them into her home. Her sister, Mary, sat at the Lord's feet, listening to what he taught. But Martha was worrying over the big dinner she was preparing. She came to Jesus and said, "Lord, doesn't it seem unfair to you that my sister just sits here while I do all the work? Tell her to come and help me." But the Lord said to her, "My dear Martha, you are so upset over all these details! There is really only one thing worth being concerned about. Mary has discovered it--and I won't take it away from her." (Luke 10:38-42, NLT)*

> *Hey you crazy Evangelical, you get so bent out of shape about doing, doing, doing. But the really important thing is just looking to Jesus and beholding His beauty, His wisdom and His great love for you. So settle down and just enjoy Him. (I Charlie 8:22 NCV)*

Chapter Eleven

The Greasy, Grimy Guilties

This is my last chapter on Daily Devotionals (DD). This whole line of thought was triggered by a conversation I had with some folks about two weeks ago. But it has been on my mind and tongue for years. You see, I was born with a healthy dose of the "guilties." I struggle with a sense of guilt about almost everything in my life. You know that thing in the Middle East? It was probably my fault! I don't know how, but I feel like I should have done more to prevent it. You get the idea. Anyway, take someone who feels guilty a lot and place him in a sub-culture that tends to thrive on guilt (in some form or another) and you have the recipe for Crazy Cake! This has been the story of much of my life in Evangelicalism. Jesus loves and saved you but in order to REALLY make Him happy, you must get-your-butt-in-gear and do the right things. Of course, one of those things is DD.

Shakin' the bones

In my heart and mind the DD ritual really became a sort of Christianized VooDoo, like the witch doctor in the Tarzan movies who would shake the bones, throw them on the ground, and "read" them to see if trouble lay ahead. Many of us have had the same (unarticulated) attitude towards DD. If we have our devotions (shakin' the bones) then things will go reasonably well for the day. If we don't have time or forget to shake the bones, then it probably won't be a good day. Or if we didn't shake the bones in the morning and establish some good Mojo with the Great Spirit, then we really shouldn't think He will be all that available to us throughout the day. Tell the truth, don't you feel more comfortable shooting up those tiny, little conversational prayers during the day if you have "earned" the right to be heard by having morning devotions?

How to ignore the truth in ten easy lessons

What's going on there? Here's my take on the subject. We came to Jesus with an understanding that He loved us no matter what! That our sins were forgiven and He would never leave us. This is true. But then our consciences and our environment began to work on us. We began to think that Jesus wouldn't continue to feel the same way about us as He once did if we don't start doing the right things, reading the right books, acting the right way and talking the right lingo. You see we have no true comparison of God's love here on earth. Ninety-nine point ninety-nine per cent of our human relationships are built upon a "tit-for-tat" basis. "I'll love you and feel good about you, if you will love me as I want you to and act as I want you to." Most of our parental relationships felt that way. "Make good grades and you are loved. Make bad grades, you're a disappointment." Therefore, our consciences will not allow us to accept this Divine Love without feeling somehow indebted TO DO something to earn it. This is where Satan has his field day! This is where most of American Christianity has fallen from the Gospel into a religious moralism.

We are told by friends and leaders that if we really want to live a great Christian life then we should meet with God first thing in the morning before the day gets the best of us. Now for most of us, trying to pray for five minutes without having our minds wander in a thousand different directions is a major victory, albeit a victory we rarely see. We try meeting with God and fail over and over again because our minds wander, we are too sleepy, we have too much to do, we worry, etc. Then we decide that we should not only pray but also read His Word. Our minds still wander and our devotional times become rather defeated endeavors. So we decide that if we just bought one of those neat devotional books that had some really neat things to think about God and some really neat prayers and prayer subjects attached, then we would do OK. Continuing to ignore the Truth of the Gospel and the marvelous fact that God loves us in Christ more than we can imagine, we set out doing our duty and trying our best to make God happy and sooth our guilty conscience. This is not everyone's scenario, but I have talked to enough Christians and been a part of this subculture long enough to know that this is hitting home with some of you out there.

I love you Darling... but only if you spend thirty minutes with me each morning.

Now going back to the husband/wife analogy of the previous chapter. What if a couple were madly in love with each other but somehow the wife got this crazy idea that the husband would be in love with her ONLY if she woke-up every morning and recited a list of needs, wants and expressions of devotion to him? The wife begins to do this. She makes a mess of things (lack of concentration, mind wandering… see above) and she feels like she really is not being a very good wife. Is there a husband out there who wouldn't say,

"Honey, our relationship is much deeper than this 'thing' you've gotten in your head. You obviously are not a morning person, you somehow think I will love you more if you spend this half hour each morning with me, but it just isn't true. I cherish every minute we spend together, but when you make such a duty out of our relationship and you believe that I am so shallow that I can only love you if you do this morning ritual it hurts my feelings and actually does damage to our relationship! Lighten up and let's enjoy our love, the love we have for each other. Relax and be yourself. Talk to me but talk to me all day. Call me on the cell phone when you are lonely. Call me when you get a good idea. Call me for what you need. Anything, anytime. I will be there for you. I love you so very much."

This works for me! Can I tell you honestly that I no longer feel a burden to get up in the morning and grunt out some heavy duty prayers? Can I tell you that DD is not a "must-be-done" on my list of Christian virtues anymore? Can I tell you that I get more excited about Christ and His love for me than ever in my life? Do I EVER get up and have DD? Totally, absolutely, YES. But when I do, it is because I am so overwhelmed by His great love for me I cannot contain my praise or my prayers. Dat' dar is some good times, my friend.

Chapter Twelve

The Myth Of Self-Improvement

Time was, whenever I went into a bookstore I would head immediately to the Self-Help Section. (This obviously is showing my true colors… IT'S ALL ABOUT ME!!) But there was something more in my devotion to self-help books than a love for ME. There was also this thought in the back of my head and the back of my heart. This thought was like the remnants of a bad hang-over that plagued me all my life. (Not that I EVER had a hang-over.) The thought simply stated (in the 2nd person) is this: You are not in control, and if you could just change a few things about your life you could be in control and be really happy. So my quest for the truth in the self-help sections was actually a quest for control and happiness. (The two things are synonymous, right?) This is where the myth of self-improvement unfolds in all it's glory, or should I say 'gory'?

We want, no we NEED to get a better grip on our lives. Right? Isn't that why we are so miserable? If we could just get a better grip, more control over ourselves and our environment, we truly could live a life of JOY. This is the myth. The myth of control. You know what I find so amazing about myself and my psyche? I am still bewildered by how quickly I swallow the bait of "having control" whenever I see it demonstrated on TV. You know, the commercials or the programs that show a very together businessman walking down a hallway. He has at least three to five people around him taking notes and getting their orders for the day. He walks very fast and the others struggle to keep up both physically and mentally. The man is spouting insightful commands and orders like he is a cross between Confusious and a drill sergeant. As he leaves his entourage and walks toward the gate at the airport, they are still writing and comparing notes on what the master has just said. I see that and I WANT TO BE THAT MAN!!!! Now there is a man in control and full of life! He has everything figured out and knows just what to do at the right time. He is cautious yet reckless because he knows that he can handle any problems that come his way. He not only has his life figured out but he provides leadership and sterling examples for his friends and employees. Now that's living!

Or perhaps for you women, you have the idol of the all together mom and career woman; a woman who sews her own clothes (size 6), bakes her own bread, is VP of sales at an advertising agency, her house is spic & span, she is on-time picking up the kids from school everyday (because she woke-up at 4:30am to do administrative work for the agency) and is head of the PTO. She sings in the choir, volunteers at the homeless shelter, brings the best dishes to all the potluck dinners and then calls you to see if there is anything she can help you with in her spare time. Besides wanting to kill this woman, we also worship her. We worship the control and smoothness she has in her life.

We all know these types of people. The media places them before us everyday. And folks, we bite the apple every time. We fall for this lie. This type of idol worship reaches into our souls and we find ourselves in lust once again. Lusting for the abilities to have it all together. Lusting for control. Lusting for the abilities to take life on. Or as a famous radio personality puts it, "Go take on the day!"

It just ain't happenin'...

Do I need to tell you that self-improvement is a fantasy of our flesh? Or have you been to enough seminars and started enough exercise routines or made enough vows to realize that we fall on our faces every time? Ruth and I perform for an annual conference on learning about applying the truths of the Gospel to our lives. The conference is growing year by year. Sometimes when I am able to speak at this conference, I tell the attendees that this conference will NOT "work" for them. It will NOT be the conference where they figure it all out and are able to go home feeling like they have a handle on living. The Gospel is NOT about control and living a regimented life. The truth of Christianity lies in the wonderful fact that no one is "all together" and we all need a Savior.

Think about it. Who were the folks that appeared to be the most together in Jesus' day? Who had their theology down and their lives regimented to conform with that theology? You guessed it. The Pharisees! And aren't we longing for that same thing in our lives? Don't we want to be in control of ourselves and our bodies and our environment to such an extent that we can kick back and glide through life knowing that we are very much like the business man mentioned above? Or like the Pharisees? Don't we want to move to that place in our lives where we really don't need faith very much? Where our prayers are much less desperate and our confidence in our flesh much higher? Isn't that really

what we are longing for when we reach for self-improvement knowledge?

So the question arises: "Would you rather be all together,
or would you rather walk close to Jesus like a shuffling,
bewildered, dense, dumb disciple–like Peter or James or
John?" And I'm guessing, other questions arise in your
mind: "Why do we want to improve?" "Are you trying to
say that living a well-disciplined life is not a life of faith?"

It is important to understand that fruitfulness and growth are the results of focusing on Christ and desiring to honor Him. When growth and change are our primary goals, we tend to be preoccupied with ourselves instead of with Christ. "Am I growing? Am I getting any better? Am I more like Christ today? What am I learning?" This inordinate preoccupation with self-improvement parallels our culture's self-help and personal enhancement movement in many ways. Personal development is certainly not wrong, but it is mis-leading--and it can be very disappointing—to make it our preeminent goal.... As we grasp the unconditional love, grace, and power of God, then honoring Christ will increasingly be our consuming passion....The only One worthy of our preoccupation is Christ, our sovereign Lord, who told Paul, "My grace is sufficient for you, for My power is perfected in weakness." ~Robert McGee

Chapter Thirteen

Self-Improvement: The New God Of The Millennium

Actually, self-improvement has been worshiped for quite some time now. But as we entered the new millennium, self-improvement went from being a past-time to being an expected, demanded pursuit for everyone. If you are not currently working hard at self-improvement then you really aren't "with it."

This attitude is very present in the Christian arena, where our holiness is measured by our busyness. After all, we must work hard and strive against the flesh to be the kind of person God wants us to be, the church wants us to be, our spouse wants us to be and our Bible study wants us to be. Therefore, we must improve. We must try harder. When we add to this agenda of "Christian" self-improvement the secular self-improvements mentioned above we now have all the ingredients for the "I-Don't-Give-a-Damn" syndrome. Or perhaps for the faint of heart we should call it the "watch spring" syndrome. You see it is my contention that all legalists and up-tight, anal-retentive types are like watches that have been wound way too tight! In the old days when we had wind-up watches and clocks, there was a chance of being too conscientious in winding them. Once a watch was wound too tightly it would break the spring inside and the spring would snap, unravel and ruin the watch. This is what happens with human beings, but especially Christians, when they are wound ever tighter and tighter until finally the spring breaks. They give-up on what they have known as "the faith" and just say, "I don't give a damn." You have seen this play out again and again with Christians in your churches and with Christians in the spot-light. I do believe that this all starts with a fervent desire, no, an obsession with self-improvement–for Jesus, of course.

Obsessing over self

Just the other day Ruth was listening to a commercial that was advertising a set of videos and books from Billy Graham. In marketing this set of works, the advertiser said, "The summary of the teaching of the Apostle Paul is this: to do good works. Therefore, we invite you to purchase this set so you may…" Ruthie, being the grace freak that she is, came into the study and told me about it. I made the comment then and I stand by it now: 99 percent of the Christians out there would have no problem with this summation. And that is a tragedy. The summary of the Apostle Paul's teaching was NOT to do good works!! This is such a heresy I hardly know where to begin. (Do not misunderstand. I am not accusing Billy Graham of heresy, just the Madison Avenue marketing firm trying to hawk these videos.) But for now let me state the obvious here: an obsession with "doing the right things" is an obsession with self.

Once again, I take my case to the example of the Pharisees! These folks were obsessed with doing the "right" things. Their minds, their hearts and their energies were centered squarely upon self as they sought to do the "righteous" works that their subculture demanded of them and they demanded of themselves. Yet Jesus came along and exposed them for the twisted, self-absorbed fools that they were. Could it be that Jesus could walk into our Christian gatherings and expose us for the same things? Could it possibly be that, like the Pharisees, we look at our "faith" as one long list of commands? "Of course not," we respond! We are too savvy to be caught by that one. We know that it is faith alone that saves us and Christianity is not a list of "Do's & Don'ts." But I would have you look behind the knee-jerk reaction which you have been conditioned to respond with. Rather look at your life and look at your fears. Look at your time alone with God. Could it be that you have been caught in the net of doing, doing, doing, doing more for God?

For the next several chapters I will be exploring this matter in more detail. So for now I would like to leave you with a few questions:

• What was wrong with the self-improvement of the Pharisees?

• What is the summary of Paul's teaching?

• Does God love you more when you have done all the right things?

• Since it is impossible to do ALL the right things, at

what point does God begin to love you less? When you have only done 60 percent of the right things? Perhaps He will start loving you less when you have only done 40 percent of the right things. How about only 20 percent?

• Where is the list of all the right things?

• How much self-improvement do you need in your life to make you really happy with yourself?

• How much self-improvement do you need in your life to feel like a more worthy person?

• Where are Jesus and faith in your gift of righteousness; in your desire to for self-improvement?

Chapter Fourteen

Self-Improvement
Or How To Live Life Without Jesus

This book has been a struggle of desire and discipline for me. I delay, procrastinate, find excuses and try to avoid the hard work of getting this book written whenever I can. I am an absolute muddle of inconsistency. However, I am now ready to make a New Year's Resolution to be more faithful... NOT!! No, but I am asking God and looking to Jesus to aid me and undertake for me in this book.

Which brings me right to THE POINT...

In the past few chapters I have been attacking the myth of self-improvement. And if you don't think self-improvement is a myth, then you are probably too proud and too busy to be reading this book anyway! But I will continue my essay in spite of your lack of attention.

For starters, let's revisit the first paragraph on this page. What is wrong with making a resolution to be better? Why not vow to try harder? Well, this approach works for some people, but I don't think it is the attitude Christians should have. WHAT??? Christians shouldn't try harder? We shouldn't vow to be better? Bingo! Let's explore.

Word from God: STOP TRYING HARDER!

Let's take a slice of life from Jane Doe. Jane has a problem with gossip. She finds herself on the phone talking with friends, gushing with rumors and judgmental condescension almost daily. She has been convicted about how wrong this is. Jane goes to God in prayer:

> "Lord, I know gossiping is wrong. Please forgive me. But I am going to try harder than ever to stop this sin and I promise to do better and be better from now on. In Jesus name. Amen."

Jane resolves to stop gossiping. She avoids her morning phone call to Sally just to avoid the temptation. It is 11 a.m. and the phone rings. It is Joan. Jane has not talked to Joan for a while and during the conversation she finds that there are so many issues upon which Joan needs to be "brought-up-to-speed." She begins to tell her about Sam and Doris and their eminent divorce. She tells her about Brenda Smith and the way she dresses like a floozy when coming to church. She talks about the outrageous behavior of that Drama Team the church hired for the Outreach Dinner. She salivates over the news that the pastor of First Church downtown had to resign due to immoral acts—which everyone thinks is a pornography addiction. And on and on and on.

Jane says goodbye to Joan and hangs up the phone. Suddenly a very large, painful pang of guilt hits her. She has just spent the last hour gossiping! She cringes. She feels so guilty. She remembers her vow to God. She clenches her fists and says, "I'm gonna try harder!" And so she renews her resolve and vows to try harder.

Later in the day, she has another phone call; she is mindful of her resolve. She almost makes it through the whole call when the other person mentions Brenda Hobbs and the flood gates are opened once again. In the midst of her conversation Jane realizes she is gossiping again, and says to herself, "Oh no, I'm doing it again! I have got to try harder!!" She ends the phone call. She sits still for a few moments and begins to think of ways she can keep her vow and stop this gossiping. She plans various methods. She contemplates having the telephone disconnected. She fantasizes about how good it will feel when she is gossip-free and she can go to God with a clear conscience. Oh, what a day that will be!

Where is Jesus?

If we are honest with ourselves (and we very rarely are) we will admit that WE are Jane Doe. We may have different issues, but the formula is the same: conviction which leads to resolution which leads to failure which leads to reaffirmation of resolution which leads to detailed schemes of how to be better. More failure. Some successes. More failure. But the pattern repeats itself over and over again. Now in examining this routine, the question I would like to ask Jane is this: Where is Jesus in your resolving and trying harder? Or to put it another way, did Jesus come for "try-harders" or did

He come for sinners? Is your resolve to be "better" a stronger potion than the blood of Christ? In other words, what really changes us? Is it our strategies of trying harder or is it faith in the Son of God to change us?

You idiot!
Are you saying we do nothing to be better? Just believe???

You idiot, right back atcha! Why is it we give FAITH such short shrift? Is FAITH an action or is it just a faint hope in the back of your head? Well, I hope to explore this issue in the coming chapters. How do we change? Where is the power to change? Is being "better" a goal that the Christian should have? Tune-in for the next chapter... if I have the discipline to write it.

Those who think they can do it on their own end up obsessed with measuring their own moral muscle but never get around to exercising it in real life. Those who trust God's action in them find that God's Spirit is in them—living and breathing God! Obsession with self in these matters is a dead end; attention to God leads us out into the open, into a spacious, free life. Focusing on the self is the opposite of focusing on God. Anyone completely absorbed in self ignores God, ends up thinking more about self than God. That person ignores who God is and what he is doing. And God isn't pleased at being ignored. ~Eugene Peterson, Romans 8, The Message

Chapter Fifteen

If I Don't Try Harder, How Do I Change?

This really is the crux of the matter. This is the question that will determine your orientation to faith and sanctification. As I have witnessed it, Evangelicals have two different theologies: 1) Learned Theology; 2) Practical Theology. Learned Theology (LT) is that theology which is taught to you by your pastors, teachers, books and most importantly, the Bible. Whereas Practical Theology (PT) is the theology you live. For example, our LT tells us not to fear because God loves us and will care for us. But our PT shows in the fact that we drive ourselves crazy with worry and phobias about our circumstances. Time and life-changes will show which theology we really own and live out of. Hopefully our

PT will become the same as our LT but this is a life-long struggle against the flesh and its old habits.

So now we come to the question, "How Does a Person Change?" And for some Christians, amazingly enough, or should I say unfortunately enough, their LT blends very nicely with their PT. Many people have been taught by their pastors and teachers: Try Harder! Organize a program! Get busy! Get your act together and start acting like you love Jesus!! Want to stop being a gossip? Then avoid long conversations. Only talk about the weather. Only talk about good things. Memorize some Bible verses about gossiping! Do it! Just DO IT!! You know the type; you know the drill. Then you also know the PT of these people. They maintain a highly disciplined (yet inwardly frenetic) lifestyle which results in a self-righteous, anal-retentive, fake, syrupy-sweet personality– otherwise known as "the Christian Personality." This is a personality that is "nice," "gentle," and never says, acts or demonstrates any sort of outrageous behavior. (This personality is usually found to be false when you place a hidden video camera in his or her home and watch how they relate to their family… especially their spouse.)

This is not the time to discuss this fully, but don't you just love the disciples because they are not afraid of outrageous behaviors or statements? They wear their hearts (and their sins) on their sleeves. They want power in the Kingdom, they want things to go their way, they openly confess their ignorance about some of Jesus' teachings, they fight with one another, they fall asleep when they should pray and they turn to run when Jesus really needs them. Thank God the disciples had not been around many religious people! Thank God they were not infected and diseased with "the Christian Personality."

Many people think that they are "being a good witness" by maintaining this vanilla, sickly, "saintly" veneer, when in actuality their fake approach to life stands as a red flag of warning to all others who would dare go the way of Christianity. Want to be neutered of all strong emotions, deep laughter, bitter tears and outrageous dancing joy? Want to live a boring life stuck in the gray twilight of "respectability?" Then come and be like us! Just look at us and see the life that you too can have. Like, duh! What a great witness!!

But getting back to self-improvement... there are those Christians whose Leaned Theology is: We are changed by grace. We change as we draw closer to Jesus. We change by faith. Yet for many who adopt this Learned Theology, their life betrays a deep commitment to the PT listed above because when confronted with the monster of their flesh, these folks fall back on what they have known all their lives: Try Harder. Work Harder and It Shall Come To Pass. Sort of like, "If you build it... they will come." As Luther mentions in his Preface to the Galatians:

> But it is a very strange thing, and unknown to the world, to teach Christians not to know the Law, and to live before God as if there were no Law or wrath of God, but total grace and mercy for Christ's sake! But even though it is strange, unless one disregards the Law and is convinced in his own heart that there is no Law or wrath from God but only grace and mercy for Christ's sake, he cannot be saved because all the Law does is show us our sin.

But what if we started acting out our LT and our outward life began to exhibit our best beliefs? What would change look like then? How does the rubber meet the road? What are the detailed steps? As they say, the Devil is in the details. Well, I would like to posit the thought that God is in the details; 'cause if He isn't then all our efforts at self-improvement will end in a colossal failure. God is in the details of a second-by-second, minute-by-minute life of faith. Our Practical Theology of change and "doing right" is much more a matter of allowing God to know the general plan of our self-improvement efforts, but the details, we believe, are our area of expertise and dominion. Is it then any wonder that our self-improvement efforts so often end in defeat?

So as we go forward in learning how to change, how to become different, we want to keep in mind that God needs to be in the details. For it is in the details that the real battle is fought. Come on, let's investigate...

[Legalism] assumes that the inside of the cup is basically good, and if people would just "do" the right thing, then everything will be okay. Rules, by themselves, can provide great comfort because it appears that we can attain them by ourselves. But for Jesus, that's the problem—"ourselves." Unless you deal with "self"—with human ego—focusing on rules is like rearranging the deck chairs on the Titanic while it is sinking....Without changing the heart, obsessing over rules is like spray-painting garbage. ~Paul Miller

Chapter Sixteen

So How Do We Change? What Does It Look Like? What Does It Feel Like? And What Are The Nitty-Gritty Steps?

Hey, not so many questions at once... sheeeesh! OK, before we start talking about change, let's get one thing straight. You will never change enough (i.e. become holy enough) that you will be satisfied with yourself and your victory over the flesh. And if you do become satisfied it just means that you are consumed with pride in your accomplishments and need to change more than ever! Get the point? Hope so.

The simple yet profound answer to the question of how we change is this: We change by faith. Enough said, let's go home.

OK, OK, we'll expand upon this a bit more. However, I am reminded of a confrontation Martin Luther had with a Papist who was mocking him for dedication to faith alone. He ridiculed Luther for opting out of the "hard work" of sanctification in exchange for "faith." Luther turned upon his accuser abruptly and shouted, "Try it for just ONE HOUR!! For one hour, try living your life as though God really does love you and will always take care of you. Try to live as if there were no reasons to worry and fret because God is on your side. Try for one hour to believe that you are in possession of all the spiritual blessings promised to us by Christ." And the conversation went further but you see his position. Faith is not some easy-believism. It is not some general nod in God's direction; a faint hope that maybe He will work on your behalf. To quote Luther once again,

> Faith is a living, daring, confidence in the grace of God. It is so certain that a man would die for it a thousand times over. This confidence and knowledge of divine grace makes a person happy, bold and of high spirits.

So to take our simple answer and expand upon it just a wee bit: we change by a living, daring confidence in the grace of God. This is the essence of change. This is how we are transformed.

Now I can hear many people shout, "What about the commands? What about the directives and imperatives given by the Apostle Paul and others? We change by JUST DOING IT!!" Happily, I must disagree. Are there directives in Scripture? Of course. Are we cajoled and commanded to get many things done and change our lives from sin and self to God and holiness? You betcha! But WHY ARE WE SO INCLINED to read these directives in the same way a Buddhist would read his list of commands and proverbs? The Evangelical church has made "doing" synonymous with "believing." And this is the reason we have so disenchanted the world and all those who have left the church in disgust. We have talked the talk of FAITH, but we have pounced upon our people with guilt and obligations to DO more and BE better.

Now ask yourself, should there be a difference in how a Christian does works of mercy and how a Buddhist does works of mercy? Should there be a difference in how a Christian spends his time in prayer and how Buddhist spends his time in prayer? Before you answer, think about the importance the Evangelical church has placed on "Just doing it!" Think of the remedies given for many problems: memorize more Scripture; become more involved in the church; witness to others more; read your Bible more; have longer devotionals, etc., etc. Have you ever gone to a Christian leader with a life or behavioral problem and the remedy given is: "Believe. Confidently lay hold of how much God loves you." Not many of us have experienced such a response.

The only qualification for the gift of the Gospel is to be dead. You don't have to be smart. You don't have to be good. You don't have to be wise. You don't have to be wonderful. You don't have to be anything…you just have to be dead. That's it. You see, the whole problem with the Church is that the Church does not want to die. None of us wants to die. But that is the one qualification and that is what is outrageous. There can be only one requirement and it's got to be low enough to include all of us…and it is. All you have to do is die. ~Robert Farrar Capon

Chapter Seventeen

How To Attain Your Goal

We have been discussing how to improve yourself. My title here refers to Paul's question in Galatians 3:3.

Are you so foolish? After beginning with the Spirit, are you now trying to attain your goal by human effort?

So what was the goal the Galatians were attempting to attain? The Galatians were trying to win the favor of God by self-improvement; by trying harder. Their goal was to be good for God so He would be happy with them–really happy. So Paul's question to them is this:

I would like to learn just one thing from you: Did you receive the Spirit by observing the law, or by believing what you heard? (Galatians 3:2, NIV)

The New Charlie Translation of that verse would read

something like this: Ok, you bunch of anal-retentive types, just tell me this: did you receive God's favor and receive the Spirit because you went to the right Bible studies, read the right books, had perfect attendance at church, memorized 389 Scripture verses, witnessed to eighty-eight people in one month and had three-hour Quiet Times sixty-six days in a row? OR was it because you believed that Christ came for sinners, of which you are the worst, and that His record of righteousness (His perfect record of right standing before God) is now your record as you believe by faith? Does God love you for what you get accomplished or does He love you because you run to Him as your loving Daddy by faith?

The Dogs of God

Let's re-visit my dogs once again. We have three dogs: Java, Mocha and Bear. Java is the Rottweiler. I know what you're thinking, "Oh no! Those are vicious dogs! How can you own one of those dogs?" Well, we felt the same way until one day someone called us on the phone to tell us that they had picked up a stray puppy wandering in the road. They had tried to find the owners but had no success. They did not have the resources to care for a dog and wanted to know if we were interested. I said "no." They then suggested that they at least bring the puppy by our house so we could tell others what it looked like, etc. Hey, these folks were no dummies!! Of course, as soon as we saw the puppy we fell in love. We kept him.

There are other stories about Java's beginning life at our house but let me skip ahead. Java is a good dog. He has mastered many commands. He does some things wrong and is sometimes a pain-in-the-lower-backside! But you know what grabs my heart? You know what really makes me love Java (probably more than the other dogs but please don't tell them)? Java has this wonderful habit of coming to me wherever I am and loving me. If I am at my desk, like now, or if I am in the easy chair or if I am reading in the living room, Java will come to me and place his (huge) doggie head in my lap and just enjoy being next to me. Even if I don't pat his head or stroke him, he will stay there just to be close to his master. There are no "good doggie works" that Java could do that would impress me more than this. This action of faith in my love for him melts my heart. Do I still want Java to obey me and do the right things around the house? Of course. But what has my heart is his desire to love and be loved by me.

Well folks, we are the dogs of God. We are the "vicious" dogs who most people would say are worthless yet God took us in off the streets and adopted us. We are the ones who gain the Master's heart by going to Him and placing our heads in His lap, just to be loved.

Be Purina Pure and Proud!

Getting back to Java. What if Java did not come and place his head in my lap but rather started to tell me all the ways he was going to be a better dog? He tells me he has sent off to Purina Dog Chow for that new study on how to be a Purina Pure and Proud Dog. He is not gonna settle for being a K-9 any longer, he is going to be a K-10!! He details for me all the ways he is going to change; the steps he is going to take and how much better he is going to be in just a few short weeks. "Just you wait and see."

Now, I've got to admit, as a mere mortal I would be somewhat impressed with Java's resolve but I would know that dogs can't really do all the things he is expecting of him-self. Furthermore, I would feel like he was taking several steps away from me emotionally. Whereas once he would come to me, trust in my love for him and revel in it, he is now so worried about himself and his doggie standing before me that his love has turned into a fearful determination to be a better dog. Now folks, I love Java but let's face it, he is a dog! He will always be a dog. There is nothing he can do to make me think he is not a dog. I am not looking for his doggie improvement. I am looking for his affection and faith in my love for him.

So the question remains: Does God send his spirit to you because you do such good doggie works and make such great doggie vows to be better? Or is it because you believe in His great love for you? What do you think melts his heart more? This is the crux of sanctification.

Chapter Eighteen

Why Do You Want To Change?

In our discussion of self-improvement, we have sort of glossed over one of the primary issues. WHY? What is motivating you to change? Is it a desire to be more holy? Before you give in to that knee-jerk reaction of saying "Yes, of course!" let's explore just a little bit. And before we explore, let me quickly give you the five-cent version of what I believe about human nature. I believe that we (in our natural state, in our flesh) are an inter-connected network of sin and sin patterns. Because of Adam, we are all born into sin and will have to deal with the sin nature all of our lives. Even Christians who have experienced the New Birth, must deal with the patterns and habits of the flesh which will constantly run toward evil and deception. This deception is nowhere more apparent than when a person looks at his own heart, life and/or motives. As Jeremiah 17 says, "The heart is desperately wicked... who can understand it?"

So, now that you understand that you can NOT understand your own heart (without the help of God) I would like
to ask you once again, why do you want to change?

Can we talk?

I cannot answer for you, but I have a sneaky suspicion
that many of my issues might also fit you fine. Let me briefly
list some of the reasons I want to change and be a better person.

- To gain the admiration of others

- To be an impressive model of Christian maturity

- To keep from doing stupid things in public

- To keep from doing stupid things in private

- To feel better about myself before God

- To be "right" and look "right" in front of my spouse

- To be a superior person

- To have the upper-hand in life

- To be one of the few, the proud, The Together People

- To feel more deserving of grace and mercy

- To maintain my fantasy of myself and my abilities

- To rise above all this repentance and confession junk

Does any of this sound familiar? I hope so; I hate being the only naked person at a formal reception, but that's another story. Of course, in our hearts and souls there is the God-given, holy desire to want to change and be more like Jesus, but I am merely listing some of the pollutants that mess up that desire and squelch it. We very rarely see the pollutants, but rather many of us think that 99 percent of our motives to change come from our desire for holiness.

You know, it's sort of like hearing on the news report that the Air Quality Index is at dangerous levels but you look out your window and the air looks fine. Beyond your ability to see (without outside help) are millions of particles of dust, soot, pollen and chemicals that could truly cause you harm. So it is, with our desire for holiness. Without the Spirit of God, we look at our motivations and they look pure, yet floating all around us are these sneaky little particles of self-ishness, self-aggrandizement, superiority and self-righteous-ness bringing our Spiritual Quality Index into the RED zone!!

Do we really want radical change?

We can know that most of our desires to change arise from selfish motives because so few of us really want a life of total sacrifice and suffering. We all want the wisdom and knowledge of the Apostle Paul, yet none of us are prepared to have such a "dismal" life. Who wants to wander from city to city being hated by thousands of people? Who wants to be whipped and beaten for the Gospel? Who wants to be so sold-out to Christ that their lives would be 180 degrees different from the relative ease and comfort of the one they are living now? We want to change but not too much. We want to be different but not too different. All this is getting too convicting for me as I sit here in an air-conditioned home is suburbia typing on my ultra-modern computer, but I hope you get the point. We are such an interconnected network of sins and fleshly motives it is difficult to truly see the how and why of desires for change. So is it any wonder that when God truly does start changing us through suffering and trials we scream back at him, "This is NOT what I had in mind!!"

We wanted to change our outbursts of anger, so we thought God would simply give us the Magic Wand of Peacefulness that we could wave whenever we were tempted to be angry. Instead, God goes deeper and starts to make our lives uncontrollable in order to humble us. Because at it's core, anger is really our frustration at not being able to control any and/or all situations. We pray for deliverance from lust, thinking that God will give us unearthly abilities of will power. Yet God may begin to expose our desire to be worshiped and adored by others which is one of the core sins of lust. Or perhaps some hard-hitting realities will be placed in our lives to allow us to see how unreal our fantasy world is.

Change is suffering and vice versa

We pray for change yet He is the One who knows what and how to change us. I find that we are most concerned about those sins that show us to be "flawed" people yet God is most concerned with those sins that show us to be self-centered, self-loving God-haters in our flesh. These are tough sins to deal with and they hardly ever are dealt with in the way we want them to be. They are deeply rooted and many times are rooted-out by tumult and violence in our lives and hearts. When we "signed-onto" Christ and into His service, did we really count the cost? Did you know that suffering and tribulation were part of the deal? If you answered no to that question, then let me break it to you gently: you will suffer if you serve. Jesus said that we will have loads of tribulation in this world, but that we should be comforted to know He has overcome the world.

When Ananias was sent to Paul, he was told by Christ that He would show Paul what he must suffer for His name. Is it any different for you and me? Why do we constantly assume that suffering is abnormal to the victorious Christian life? Did Paul live a life of victory? Of course! Was he a success? Of course not! Not in the way we measure success in ministry today. Did he have a huge church? Did he have a nice home and car–er… chariot? Did he have thousands of people on his mailing list? Did he have a TV ministry? Did he video tape all occasions of ministry for a fund raiser on his TV show? Could he number his conversions? His books? His Bible Study series?

I bring all this up NOT to make us feel guilty–although I feel pretty sheepish about my ambitions in ministry. But I want us to get honest with God and honest with ourselves. Do we really want to change? Do we really want an abundant life of suffering? Do we really want God to have His way with us or do we want God to have OUR way with us?

In the next chapter we will look at our motivations and the reasons we choose to focus-in on certain aspects of change in our lives but stay away from others. For today, won't you please just take a few moments, look out the window and ask God to show you the REAL state of the "air" around you

Chapter Nineteen

At Best, We're All Cracked Pots

One of my favorite author's is Brennan Manning. Ruth and I have just finished his book, *Ruthless Trust*. It is this book that God used to bring me out of my latest funk of soul. I want to quote from Chapter 10 entitled "The Cracked Pot." Enjoy.

> A water-bearer in India had two large pots. Each hung on opposite ends of a pole that he carried across his neck. One of the pots had a crack in it, while the other was perfect. The latter always delivered a full portion of water at the end of the long walk from the stream to the master's house. The cracked pot arrived only half-full. Every day for a full two years, the water-bearer delivered only one and a half pots of water.
>
> The perfect pot was proud of its accomplishments, because it fulfilled magnificently the purpose for which it had been made. But the poor cracked pot was ashamed of its imperfection, miserable that it was able to accomplish

only half of what it had been made to do.

After the second year of what it perceived to be a bitter failure, the unhappy pot spoke to the water-bearer one day by the stream.

"I am ashamed of myself, and I want to apologize to you," the pot said.

"Why?" asked the bearer. "What are you ashamed of?"

"I have been able, for these past two years, to deliver only half my load, because this crack in my side causes water to leak out all the way back to your master's house. Because of my flaws, you have to do all this work and you don't get full value from your efforts," the pot said.

The water-bearer felt sorry for the old cracked pot, and in his compassion, he said, "As we return to the master's house, I want you to notice the beautiful flowers along the path." Indeed, as they went up the hill, the cracked pot took notice of the beautiful wildflowers on the side of the path, bright in the sun's glow, and the sight cheered it up a bit.

But at the end of the trail, it still felt bad that it had leaked out half its load, and so again it apologized to the bearer for its failure.

The bearer said to the pot, "Did you notice that there were flowers only on your side of the path, not on the other pot's side? That is because I have always known about your flaw, and I have taken advantage of it. I planted flower seeds on your side of the path, and every day, as we have walked back from the stream, you have watered them. For two years I have been able to pick these beautiful flowers to decorate my master's table. Without you being just the way you are, he would not have had this beauty to grace his house."

Eager to extract a moral from this lovely story, the artist of the obvious will hasten to tell us that we are all cracked pots and that we should allow Jesus to use our flaws in order to grace his Father's table. Such trite moralizing spoils the story. Using the cracked pot to serve his didactic purpose, the moralist preens his feathers by laying another burden on us, saying, in effect, "Accept your clumsy, cockeyed selves, you dimwitted dorks!"

Unquestionably, a moral code is indispensable for an

authentic spiritual life. We are intellectually, aesthetically, and morally ill to the extent that we lack firm rootedness in ultimate reality. We are by essence transcendent beings, and as such we cannot live fully without a solid, secure commitment to values, morals, and goals.

However, incessant and exclusive moralizing reduces the Good News to a tedious behavioral code, a rigid ethic, or an altruistic philosophy of life…

…The water-bearer stunned the cracked pot with the words,

"Without you the Master would not have had this beauty to grace his house." The pot had assumed that the sole purpose of its existence was to haul water from the stream to the house. Enfolded within its narrow self-determination, the flawed pot had not suspected God's grand purpose for it; to give life to the dormant flower seeds along the path.

Does not this restricted view describe our own situation? We formulate plans to fulfill what we perceive to be the purpose of our lives (inevitably limited), and when the locomotive of our longings gets derailed, we deem ourselves failures.

Brennan Manning, Ruthless Trust. Hardcover - 190 pages 1 Ed edition (October 2000) Harper San Francisco; ISBN: 0062517090

So how and why do we want to change?

Does the parable above hit you between the eyes? It hits me. As I seek change in my life, I ignore what God is doing in and through my weaknesses. I become so discouraged at my ineptitudes and stupidity. I want to change to be more competent, more able to fulfill the role that I have chosen for my life. But perhaps I should just ease-up and relax in the role that God has chosen for me. A very wise minister of the Gospel once remarked that the true sign of discipleship is making a fool of yourself in public. What???? No, that can't be right! But look at the disciples. They are the ones always

saying the wrong things, doing the dumb things, and showing NO spiritual wisdom at all! Yet look at the Pharisees…
they were competent, "together" and very efficient. So could
it be that I want to be more and more like a Pharisee? Yes!
You see, the disciples lived on the edge. They made mistakes
because they LIVED LIFE with Jesus and they risked everything to find out what this Kingdom of God is all about. Of
course they were going to make mistakes, make fools of
themselves in front of God and everybody! But the Pharisees
were those people who took no risks. They lived in the safe-
ty of the black and white, rigid rules of the Law (and some
bizarre interpretations of that Law). They sought to NOT
look foolish in public. Yet guess what, in reality they looked
much more foolish than the Crack Pot Disciples.

So we come back to the issue of change and WHY? The
real issue is: why. Do you want to be more holy? Or do you
just want to be more together in public? Do you want to
change because you want to live a life of love and grace, or
is it because you want to live a life of moral efficiency and
function?

Chapter Twenty

Changing... Let's Just Do It!

In our zeal to change our lives, habits, tendencies and sin patterns we almost inevitably run to the wrong source. We run to the Law and the imperatives of Scripture. We grasp onto the mythical, fantastic promise of the flesh which vows that it can be better, do better and perform better. We believe the flesh. We make resolutions. We make vows. We promise ourselves and our families and our God that improvement is just 'round the bend. We return to the Nike Christianity we have known for years: Just Do It!... for Jesus, of course. In a few weeks or months we find ourselves either overwhelmed with our inabilities to maintain our vows or dripping with a slick coating of self-righteousness for "toughing it out." Oh sure, we nearly always remember to tack-on an "Amen" or "In the Name of Jesus" to our resolves, but the fact remains we run to the Slave Master and not the Liberator.

The truth shall set you free...
Yeah, right.

Our very good friend and mentor Steve Brown offers a weekend retreat for churches called "Born Free." This weekend is a life-giving time of teaching, laughing, singing and learning more about grace and our freedom in Christ. However, this retreat has often been a "hard sell." The reason being that most Christians are convinced they are free! Do I have to tell you what a bunch of up-tight, anal-retentive types populate the Christian church in America? Would you characterize the Evangelical World as a bunch of fun-loving, happy, free folks? Well, if you are honest with yourself you would have to say, "NO!!!" Yet we are told over and over again by our leaders and our teachers that we are "free." Therefore, when Steve tries to get people interested in the "Born Free" retreat they shake their heads knowing that they don't need that kind of stuff.

However, we all know what "sells" in the Christian community. What really sells are "How to..." retreats, books and seminars. If Steve were to rename his retreat "The Ten Laws of Freedom and How to Implement Them in Your Life" people would be flocking to the doors! You see, we long to have definitive answers. We would pay good money to have someone tell us what to do and when to do it. We would much rather have the black & white rules of the law in front of us than the ONE scary Rule of Love.

The mechanics of changing

We have talked about what change is NOT and we have examined our motives for change. At long last I want to reveal The List:

List of Requirements for Change in Your Life

1. Draw close to Jesus.

I'll pause here for just a moment to allow you to take notes and copy this long list on a piece of paper.............

Almost done? No? I'll wait while you write.............

Finished? Ok, just a minute more............

I'm sorry we need to move on. If you have to, come back later and finish copying this long list.

Well, I am being just a bit facetious, but in reality this is the truth that sets us free. I love this verse in Acts:

> *"When they saw the courage of Peter and John and realized that they were unschooled, ordinary men, they were astonished and they took note that these men had been with Jesus." (Acts 4:13, NIV)*

I do not want to site "proof texts" just to make my point, but I do think that it is a general, spiritual rule of thumb that people change as they encounter the Almighty. Just as Moses' face shone and beamed dramatically from his conversations with God, so our lives radiate joy and peace as we draw close to Him. Unschooled, ordinary men and women become extraordinary as they are exposed to Jesus. The goofs are gladiators; the stupid are stupendous; sinners shine with forgiveness and the doubtful become daring.

The real list...
Write this one down!

Now I have been in the Evangelical community long enough to know that there are some really, REALLY corrupt concepts of Jesus out there. I know because I struggled for years with a corrupt view of Jesus. So for some of you, when I say "Draw close to Jesus," it is tantamount to saying, "Go hug that old, bitter uncle of yours who watches you day and night for some inkling of goodness in you and who is VERY disappointed in what he sees in your life and behavior."

So I feel compelled to write a list. The real list of things that should make Jesus attractive to you. For starters let's go here:

The Jesus List:

If I speak in the tongues of men and of angels, but have not Jesus,

I am only a resounding gong or a clanging cymbal.

If I have the gift of prophecy and can fathom all mysteries and all knowledge, and if I have a faith that can move mountains, but have not Jesus, I am nothing.

If I give all I possess to the poor and surrender my body to the flames, but have not Jesus, I gain nothing.
Jesus is patient,
Jesus is kind.
He does not envy,
He does not boast,
He is not proud.
He is not rude,
He is not self-seeking,
He is not easily angered,
He keeps no record of wrongs.
Jesus does not delight in evil but rejoices with the truth.
He always protects, always trusts, always hopes, always perseveres.
Jesus never fails.
And now these three remain: faith, hope and Jesus. But the greatest of these is Jesus. (1 Corinthians 13:1-13, NIV with obvi-

ous substitutions)

When Jesus saw their faith, he said to the paralytic, 'Take heart, son; your sins are forgiven.'"(Matthew 9:2, NIV)

When he heard this, Jesus replied, "Healthy people don't need a doctor--sick people do." (Matthew 9:12, NLT)

Jesus turned around and said to her, "Daughter, be encouraged! Your faith has made you well." And the woman was healed at that moment. (Matthew 9:22, NLT)

Then Jesus said, "Come to me, all of you who are weary and carry heavy burdens, and I will give you rest." (Matthew 11:28, NLT)

But Jesus spoke to them at once. "It's all right," he said. "I am here! Don't be afraid." (Matthew 14:27, NLT)

But Jesus said, "Let the children come to me. Don't stop them! For the Kingdom of Heaven belongs to such as these." (Matthew 19:14, NLT)

Jesus felt sorry for them and touched their eyes. Instantly they could see! Then they followed him. (Matthew 20:34, NLT)

The next morning Jesus awoke long before daybreak and went out alone into the wilderness to pray. (Mark 1:35, NLT)

Moved with pity, Jesus touched him. "I want to," he said. "Be healed!" (Mark 1:41, NLT)

When Jesus heard this, he told them, "Healthy people don't need a doctor--sick people do. I have come to call sinners, not those who think they are already good enough." (Mark 2:17, NLT)

But Jesus said, "No, go home to your friends, and tell them what wonderful things the Lord has done for you and how merciful he has been." (Mark 5:19, NLT)

But Jesus ignored their comments and said to Jairus, "Don't be afraid. Just trust me." (Mark 5:36, NLT)

Jesus looked at them intently and said, "Humanly speaking, it is impossible. But not with God. Everything is possible with God." (Mark 10:27, NLT)

When the Lord Jesus had finished talking with them, he was taken up into heaven and sat down in the place of honor at God's right hand. (Mark 16:19, NLT)

Then Jesus said to the woman, "Your sins are forgiven." (Luke 7:48, NLT)

Then Jesus took her by the hand and said in a loud voice, "Get up, my child!" (Luke 8:54, NLT)

Then Jesus was filled with the joy of the Holy Spirit and said, "O Father, Lord of heaven and earth, thank you for hiding the truth from those who think themselves so wise and clever, and for revealing it to the childlike. Yes, Father, it pleased you to do it this way." (Luke 10:21, NLT)

Jesus responded, "Salvation has come to this home today, for this man has shown himself to be a son of Abraham." (Luke 19:9, NLT)

Jesus told them, "In this world the kings and great men order their people around,... Normally the master sits at the table and is served by his servants. But not here! For I am your servant." (Luke 22:25-27, NLT)

Finally, they came to a place called The Skull. All three were crucified there–Jesus on the center cross, and the two criminals on either side. Jesus said, "Father, forgive these people, because they don't know what they are doing." (Luke 23:33,34, NLT)

For the law was given through Moses; God's unfailing love and faithfulness came through Jesus Christ. (John 1:17, NLT)

Jesus replied, "If you only knew the gift God has for you and who I am, you would ask me, and I would give you living water." (John 4:10, NLT)

Then Jesus told her, "I am the Messiah!" (John 4:26, NLT)

Jesus replied, "I assure you, the Son can do nothing by himself. He does only what he sees the Father doing. Whatever the Father does, the Son also does." (John 5:19, NLT)

Jesus told them, "This is what God wants you to do: Believe in the one he has sent." (John 6:29, NLT)

Jesus replied, "I am the bread of life. No one who comes to me will ever be hungry again. Those who believe in me will never thirst." *(John 6:35, NLT)*

So Jesus told them, "I'm not teaching my own ideas, but those of God who sent me." *(John 7:16, NLT)*

Then Jesus stood up again and said to her, "Where are your accusers? Didn't even one of them condemn you?" "No, Lord," she said. And Jesus said, "Neither do I. Go and sin no more." Jesus said to the people, "I am the light of the world. If you follow me, you won't be stumbling through the darkness, because you will have the light that leads to life." *(John 8:10-12, NLT)*

Jesus answered, "If I am merely boasting about myself, it doesn't count. But it is my Father who says these glorious things about me. You say, 'He is our God.'" *(John 8:54, NLT)*

Then Jesus told him, "I have come to judge the world. I have come to give sight to the blind and to show those who think they see that they are blind." *(John 9:39, NLT)*

Now Jesus had stayed outside the village, at the place where Martha met him. *(John 11:30, NLT)*

When Jesus saw her weeping and saw the other people wailing with her, he was moved with indignation and was deeply troubled. "Where have you put him?" he asked them. They told him, "Lord, come and see." Then Jesus wept. *(John 11:33-35, NLT)*

Jesus responded, "Didn't I tell you that you will see God's glory if you believe?" So they rolled the stone aside. Then Jesus looked up to heaven and said, "Father, thank you for hearing me." *(John 11:40,41, NLT)*

Jesus shouted to the crowds, "If you trust me, you are really trusting God who sent me." *(John 12:44, NLT)*

Then Jesus told him, "You believe because you have seen me. Blessed are those who haven't seen me and believe anyway." *(John 20:29, NLT)*

Once more he asked him, "Simon son of John, do you love me?" Peter was grieved that Jesus asked the question a third time. He said, "Lord, you know everything. You know I love you." Jesus said, "Then feed my sheep. The truth is, when you were young, you were able to do as you liked and go wherever you wanted to. But when you are old, you will stretch out *your hands, and others will direct you and take you where you don't want to go." Jesus said this to let him know what kind of death he would die to glorify God. Then Jesus told him, "Follow me." (John 21:17-19, NLT)*

We are made right in God's sight when we trust in Jesus Christ to take away our sins. And we all can be saved in this same way, no matter who we are or what we have done. For all have sinned; all fall short of God's glorious standard. Yet now God in his gracious kindness declares us not guilty. He has done this through Christ Jesus, who has freed us by taking away our sins. (Romans 3:22-24, NLT)

Therefore, since we have been made right in God's sight by faith, we have peace with God because of what Jesus Christ our Lord has done for us. (Romans 5:1, NLT.)

So now we can rejoice in our wonderful new relationship with God—all because of what our Lord Jesus Christ has done for us in making us friends of God. (Romans 5:11, NLT)

So now there is no condemnation for those who belong to Christ Jesus. (Romans 8:1, NLT)

Who then will condemn us? Will Christ Jesus? No, for he is the one who died for us and was raised to life for us and is sitting at the place of highest honor next to God, pleading for us. (Romans 8:34, NLT)

Whether we are high above the sky or in the deepest ocean, nothing in all creation will ever be able to separate us from the love of God that is revealed in Christ Jesus our Lord. (Romans 8:39, NLT)

I can never stop thanking God for all the generous gifts he has given you, now that you belong to Christ Jesus. He has enriched your church with the gifts of eloquence and every kind of knowledge. This shows that what I told you about Christ is true. Now you have every spiritual gift you need as you eagerly wait for the return of our Lord Jesus Christ. He will keep you strong right up to the end, and he will keep you free from all blame on the great day when our Lord Jesus Christ returns. (1 Corinthians 1:4-8, NLT)

God alone made it possible for you to be in Christ Jesus. For our benefit God made Christ to be wisdom itself. He is the one who made us acceptable to God. He made us pure and holy, and he gave himself to purchase our freedom. (1 Corinthians 1:30, NLT)

For I decided to concentrate only on Jesus Christ and his death on the cross. (1 Corinthians 2:2, NLT)

There was a time when some of you were just like that, but now your sins have been washed away, and you have been set apart for God. You have been made right with God because of what the Lord Jesus Christ and the Spirit of our God have done for you. (1 Corinthians 6:11, NLT)

For God, who said, "Let there be light in the darkness," has made us understand that this light is the brightness of the glory of God that is seen in the face of Jesus Christ. (2 Corinthians 4:6, NLT)

For God made Christ, who never sinned, to be the offering for our sin, so that we could be made right with God through Christ. (2 Corinthians 5:21, NLT)

You know how full of love and kindness our Lord Jesus Christ was. Though he was very rich, yet for your sakes he became poor, so that by his poverty he could make you rich. (2 Corinthians 8:9, NLT)

So you are all children of God through faith in Christ Jesus. (Galatians 3:26, NLT)

As for me, God forbid that I should boast about anything except the cross of our Lord Jesus Christ. Because of that cross, my interest in this world died long ago, and the world's interest in me is also long dead. (Galatians 6:14, NLT)

His unchanging plan has always been to adopt us into his own family by bringing us to himself through Jesus Christ. And this gave him great pleasure. (Ephesians 1:5, NLT.)

For he raised us from the dead along with Christ, and we are seated with him in the heavenly realms-all because we are one with Christ Jesus. (Ephesians 2:6, NLT)

For we are God's masterpiece. He has created us anew in Christ Jesus, so that we can do the good things he planned for us long ago. (Ephesians 2:10, NLT)

God knows how much I love you and long for you with the tender compassion of Christ Jesus. (Philippians 1:8, NLT)

But we are citizens of heaven, where the Lord Jesus Christ lives. And we are eagerly waiting for him to return as our Savior. (Philippians 3:20, NLT)

If you do this, you will experience God's peace, which is far more wonderful than the human mind can understand. His peace will guard your hearts and minds as you live in Christ Jesus. (Philippians 4:7, NLT)

And they speak of how you are looking forward to the coming of God's Son from heaven--Jesus, whom God raised from the dead. He is the one who has rescued us from the terrors of the coming judgment. (1 Thessalonians 1:10, NLT)

For God decided to save us through our Lord Jesus Christ, not to pour out his anger on us. (1 Thessalonians 5:9, NLT)

No matter what happens, always be thankful, for this is God's will for you who belong to Christ Jesus. (1 Thessalonians 5:18, NLT)

This is a true saying, and everyone should believe it: Christ Jesus came into the world to save sinners-and I was the worst of them all. (1 Timothy 1:15, NLT)

For there is only one God and one Mediator who can reconcile God and people. He is the man Christ Jesus. (1 Timothy 2:5, NLT)

And now he has made all of this plain to us by the coming of Christ Jesus, our Savior, who broke the power of death and showed us the way to everlasting life through the Good News. (2 Timothy 1:10, NLT)

What we do see is Jesus, who "for a little while was made lower than the angels" and now is "crowned with glory and honor" because he suffered death for us. Yes, by God's grace, Jesus tasted death for everyone in all the world. And it was only right that God-who made everything and for whom everything was made-should bring his many children into glory. Through the suffering of Jesus, God made him a perfect leader, one fit to bring them into their salvation. - (Hebrews 2:9,10, NLT)

(But Jesus remains a priest forever; his priesthood will never end. Therefore he is able, once and forever, to save everyone who comes to God through him. He lives forever to plead with God on their behalf. He is the kind of high priest we need because he is holy and blameless, unstained by sin. He has now been set apart from sinners, and he has been given

the highest place of honor in heaven. He does not need to offer sacrifices every day like the other high priests. They did this for their own sins first and then for the sins of the people. But Jesus did this once for all when he sacrificed himself on the cross. (Hebrews 7:24-27, NLT)

And so, dear brothers and sisters, we can boldly enter heaven's Most Holy Place because of the blood of Jesus. (Hebrews 10:19, NLT)

We do this by keeping our eyes on Jesus, on whom our faith depends from start to finish. He was willing to die a shameful death on the cross because of the joy he knew would be his afterward. Now he is seated in the place of highest honor beside God's throne in heaven. (Hebrews 12:2, NLT)

All honor to the God and Father of our Lord Jesus Christ, for it is by his boundless mercy that God has given us the privilege of being born again. Now we live with a wonderful expectation because Jesus Christ rose again from the dead. (1 Peter 1:3, NLT)

The one who existed from the beginning is the one we have heard and seen. We saw him with our own eyes and touched him with our own hands. He is Jesus Christ, the Word of life. (1 John 1:1, NLT)

But if we are living in the light of God's presence, just as Christ is, then we have fellowship with each other, and the blood of Jesus, his Son, cleanses us from every sin. (1 John 1:7, NLT)

My dear children, I am writing this to you so that you will not sin. But if you do sin, there is someone to plead for you before the Father. He is Jesus Christ, the one who pleases God completely. (1 John 2:1, NLT)

Let this encourage God's holy people to endure persecution patiently and remain firm to the end, obeying his commands and trusting in Jesus. (Revelation 14:12, NLT)

"I, Jesus, have sent my angel to give you this message for the churches. I am both the source of David and the heir to his throne. I am the bright morning star." The Spirit and the bride say, "Come." Let each one who hears them say, "Come." Let the thirsty ones come–anyone who wants to. Let them come and drink the water of life without charge... He who is the faithful witness to all these things says, "Yes, I am coming soon!" Amen! Come, Lord Jesus! (Revelation 22:16-20, NLT)

If you have lasted to the end of the Jesus List, congratulations. I have been greatly encouraged re-digesting these verses; I hope you have been, too. So when I ask you to draw close to Jesus, I am asking you to lay your head in the lap of your lover and relax. Maybe even nap awhile, knowing that even in your "sleeping" He is changing you. God bless.

Chapter Twenty-One

Yeah, Yeah...
I Already Know All That...

If you have not read the previous chapter with the Jesus List, turn back and read it now. Once you have read it, let me ask you a question: When reading through Scripture, is it your temptation (as well as mine) to briefly look at the verse or reference to the verse and then politely skip over it, saying to yourself,

"Oh, yeah. I know this passage. Right. Yep. This is the passage where Jesus forgives the guy's sins and heals him so he can walk again. Right. Got it. Next?"

This is a fairly constant temptation to us Bible Bangers. We read without reading. We see without seeing. We know without knowing. This is how we maintain such horrible ideas about Jesus and about the Kingdom of God. So what I would like you to do is this: drown yourself in the wonder of Jesus. Go back to my Jesus List and revel in who He is and note His constant return to compassion and gentleness. Allow yourself to be startled once again by the Gospel.

Hey, man... Can ya spare some change?

I know that there might be some out there who have been waiting for the list of things to do in order to see change in their lives. I hope I have totally frustrated you. There is no list. There is just one law. That is the Law of Love.

In years past, I would have been angered by that last statement. It has no meaning, right? What do I mean by the "Law of Love?" Well, folks this is the dividing line between the men and boys. It separates the women from the girls. The Dobermans from the Pekineses. The Suburbans from the Yugos. The Trinitarians from the Monotheists. We claim to be Trinitarian in our theology, yet our lives rarely reflect that reality. This could fall under the category of "you have not because you ask not." I mean, we have the Spirit of God. The law is written on our hearts. Our old heart of stone has been removed and we have been given a new heart of flesh. God's Holy Spirit has been given to us to guide and to walk alongside us. Yet for most of us, we act like the Spirit was never given.

The Spirit of God is to lead us to truth, hence to Christ. We have the Spirit as a guarantee from God that this whole Christianity thing is true. But if we are really honest with ourselves we might cry out that if the Spirit is the guarantee, we want to negotiate another contract because this a pretty intangible guarantee of an even more intangible promise! That is because we live much of our inner life in loneliness. We are alone because we forget to trust the Spirit and rely on His leading. I love the passage:

> *For everyone who asks, receives. Everyone who seeks, finds. And the door is opened to everyone who knocks. You fathers–if your children ask for a fish, do you give them a snake instead? Or if they ask for an egg, do you give them a scorpion? Of course not! If you sinful people know how to give good gifts to your children, how much more will your heavenly Father give the Holy Spirit to those who ask him. (Luke 11:10-13, NLT)*

Jack Miller brought this passage to our hearts over and over again. We tend to think that the gift of the Spirit is one of those once-for-all-time things that happened when we believed but we don't really need to concern ourselves with it again. Yet here, in this passage, the Spirit of God and His presence in our lives is compared to food and gifts that we need to ask for and appreciate daily. So my question is: How often do we ask God for the Holy Spirit? How does He show Himself in our lives? How does He rank in our hearts as a leader and negotiator of truth and holiness?

The holy who?

If we are honest, most of us will have to say that the Spirit has been given little attention in our hearts and lives. Fortunately, He does continue to work in those who don't appreciate Him and in those who, for the most part, ignore Him. But let me take you to another one of my favorite Scriptures:

> *Then I will sprinkle clean water on you, and you will be clean. Your filth will be washed away, and you will no longer worship idols. And I will give you a new heart with new and right desires, and I will put a new spirit in you. I will take out your stony heart of sin and give you a new, obedient heart. And I will put my Spirit in you so you will obey my laws and do whatever I command. (Ezekiel 36:25-27, NLT)*

I guess the question here is: Do we really believe that God has done what He says He has done? Did He sprinkle us clean and give us a Spirit that will change us and allow us to obey Him?

Well… I'm waiting. Whatcha think?

Do we have a Spirit in us that will lead us to truth and holiness or is this just some flowery language to hide the fact that sanctification is really all sweat and tears and hard work and discipline? Or how about this passage:

> *I always pray for you, and I make my requests with a heart full of joy because you have been my partners in spreading the Good News about Christ from the time you first heard it until now. And I am sure that God, who began the good work within you, will continue his work until it is finally finished on that day when Christ Jesus comes back again. (Philippians 1:4-6, NLT)*

Why don't we have that same confidence? Why are we so dogged and defeated so often? I think it is because we really don't believe that God is working His will in our lives and that He will complete it until the Day of Christ. We are so uptight about the doing and the reading and the studying and the witnessing and the rebuking and the praying and the looking "right"… for Jesus, of course.

"You wouldn't be so surprised at your sin if you didn't have such a high opinion of yourself in the first place."
Steve Brown

Chapter Twenty-Two

You Do Good To God...
He Be Good To You
You Do Bad To God...
He STILL Be Good To You

Please excuse my lame attempt at ebonics but, nonetheless, it is true. Yet this is one of the most difficult concepts to understand and appreciate in all of Christian doctrine. But it has been so obvious, even from the Garden of Eden, a remarkable instance with Abraham and all the way through the Bible. I have found that if you understand this concept then all the conditional statements of the Scriptures can be understood. You know, the statements where God seems to say, "If you do this, then I will do that." Our flesh LOVES those kinds of statements! They are measurable. They depend on us and our goodness to initiate the movement. We see our religious duties and we do them, check-off the list and wait for God to come through with His part. It is this heresy that takes thousands of folks to Christian counselors every month. We expect the "right" things from God because we have done the "right" things for Him. Oh boy!! This opens a whole 'nother can of worms, but I will avoid this tempting rabbit trail for now. Back to the issue at hand: the conditional statements of Scripture.

Back to Eden

The ultimate conditional statement from God came in the first law given to humans: eat the forbidden fruit and you will die; don't eat it and you will live. Very plain. Very precise. Very conditional. Yet when we look at how the Almighty treated those people (Adam/Eve–hence you/me) who disobeyed, we can see how, even when we are bad for God, He is still good to us. You see, God did carry through on His promise of death to disobedient humans, but then as soon as He had carried out the death sentence, He immediately provided for life. He dressed their nakedness with the covering from a blood sacrifice (signifying One who would be sacrificed for us–Gen. 3:21) and also preached the Gospel to them in promising One who would one day come and crush the head of the serpent for us. (Gen. 3:15)

Consequences? Yes, there were and are consequences to our sins but the glory of grace is that, even from the beginning, God goes beyond the conditional consequences to provide mercy and love to the worst of sinners.

The sleeping covenant partner

Another example which I believe to be one of the most beautifully shocking pictures of grace is found in Genesis 15. But before I go further I must give you some background on covenants. In Genesis 15 God enters into a covenantal relationship with Abraham. In the days of Abraham, they were really into visual pictures of their dealings with one another. So if we were to make a covenant of peace between our two families, we would strike a bargain about how we would keep the covenant; which things would be allowed between us and which things would not be allowed. We would settle upon this covenant (the list of do's and don'ts) and then ratify the covenant with a visual ritual to remind us of the solemnity of our actions.

It would be a common covenant ritual for us to take animals, kill them, split them in half and lay the animal parts on the ground in a straight line. The left half of the animals on the left side, the right half of the animals on the right side. This line of animal parts would form an aisle or "hallway," of sorts, for someone to walk through. Having laid out the animal parts, we then recite the terms of the treaty. After such recitation, we would each take turns walking through the dead animal aisle and we would say something like this: "May I become as these dead, mutilated animals if I fail to keep this covenant." Anybody hungry? Pretty graphic, huh?

Well, this is the exact same ritual that God initiates with Abraham in Genesis 15. God has just promised Abraham that he would be the father of a great nation. He has said his descendants would be as numerous as the stars in the sky. Then Abraham very subtly replies, "Oh, yeah, how can I be sure that you will really keep your word?" (Gen. 15:8) It is then that God tells Abraham to get ready for the covenant ritual. He instructs him to get the animals and split them in half. They are now ready to start the ritual. But God does a strange thing. He knocks-out Abraham! Abraham is not able to walk the aisle of conditions. Instead God shows up in the form of a smoking torch and passes through the animal pieces alone! In essence what God is saying is this: "May I become like one of these animals if I fail to keep this covenant." But the astounding, nay, scandalous thing is that, in essence, He is also saying, "May I become like one of these animals if YOU fail to keep the covenant as well!!" God assumes the responsibilities and consequences for both parties!

Our Covenant Keeper and Consequence Bearer

There is, of course, much more that can be said about this passage and it's ramifications, and much more can be said about covenants and treaties in ancient times, but I want to point out that God kept His promise. When Abraham (and all of Abraham's children) failed to keep the covenant, what did God do? He came to earth and became like one of those mutilated animals. He took the consequences of our covenant breaking. He came to fulfill the just requirements of the covenant He made with Abraham!

Astounding, eh? So you see, Christian, even when you fail to keep-up your side of the bargain, God is there for you to fulfill the legal requirements of a covenant-breaker ! And it's a dreadful curse for those who disobey!

This picture of grace should excite us and relieve us from the great burden of trying to keep the law so God will be good to us. Because even if we don't keep the law, he has became like a mutilated animal and has already kept our side of the bargain.

So be like Abraham. Go to sleep and rest, accepting the shocking grace of our Covenant Keeper.

Chapter Twenty-Three

Grace For The Unaware

As I travel this road from birth to the grave in the arms of Jesus, I have become somewhat aware of how unaware I am of Him and His goodness to me. I say "somewhat aware" because even my awareness is clouded by a fog of unawareness. Uh… yeah… whatever that means. No kidding, being human or even worse than that, a fallen human, I have such a limited vision of who God is, what He is like and how He works in this universe. And even when He gives me insight through His Word and through His Spirit, I feebly forget or mishandle the messages He gives. Thus my qualification for my sense of unaware awareness.

I am convinced that the biggest part of our lives as Christians is to be brought from one state of awareness of God's glory to another. God uses our stories, our events, our dreams, our heartaches, our failures, our families, our hopes, our desires, our jobs–everything to bring about a more lasting awareness of Himself and His love for us. How this happens and why He chooses the methods He does remains a mystery, but still He desires our awareness. Yet as we gain awareness, our selfishness, dullness and sinfulness squelch this awareness almost as soon as it shows up.

This is why the Gospel is such good news to us over and over again. We keep forgetting about it but then suddenly stumble upon it again. And all we can say when we see this love of Christ again is "Wow!" But perhaps some of us don't. Perhaps we remain almost utterly unaware of His goodness, delighting instead to dwell on our needs, wants and disappointments. What happens then? What does God do? The Good News coming to us once again is that there is grace, even for the unaware. In the next few pages, I want to explore this aspect of our apprehending God and/or His interacting with us. I will be laying a foundation for our discussions, hence the writing will be a bit more theological and philosophical than it has been in the previous pages.

God's baby talk

As mentioned earlier, Calvin has said that the Bible is God's baby talk to us. When we talk to children and answer their questions, we must couch things in a way they will understand. When they ask, "How does a car run?" We don't whip out a Popular Science magazine and begin going through the details of the internal combustion engine. No, we might tell the child, "The car burns gasoline and that makes the wheels go." This is true but it is not complete in detail. It is true but the car doesn't really "burn" gasoline; it takes small quantities of petrol, injects it into a cylinder, ignites it with a spark causing a small explosion, this causes the piston in the cylinder to move, etc. Yet, when we tell the child this "dumbed down" version of how a car runs, we are telling the truth, just not completely. This is how God talks to us, which brings up an axiomatic statement that Richard Pratt drilled into my head years ago: we can know truly, even when we cannot know completely. The truth that God gives to us is not complete. Humans cannot understand the complete truth; we just don't have the capacity. Yet the knowledge we do have (that God has given us) though incomplete, can be trusted to be true. This might seem like the "angels on the head of a pin" type of distinction, but it is important to lay the groundwork for our discussion on awareness. We will never be fully aware, i.e. Godlike, but we can trust the knowledge we have been given and strive with courage to become as aware as we can of this knowledge of God and His creation. Make sense? Hope so.

Created to be aware

To read the first three chapters of Genesis is to hear a glorious but sad, sad story. It is glorious as it tells of creation, of man's relationship with God and all the created world. It is glorious as it tells of man's relationship with his wife. But it is sad as we witness the creeping death of creation through the curse of the Fall. As the consequences of the Fall descend upon mankind through the sin of Adam, one of the primary aspects of loss is his awareness of life. But I am getting ahead of myself. Let us first consider, how, in our natural, uncorrupted selves, we were created to be aware.

> Then God said, "Let us make people in our image, to be like ourselves. They will be masters over all life-the fish in the sea, the birds in the sky, and all the livestock, wild animals, and small animals." So God created people in his own image; God patterned them after himself; male and female he created them. God blessed them and told them, "Multiply and fill the earth and subdue it. Be masters over the fish and birds and all the animals." And God said, "Look! I have given you the seed-bearing plants throughout the earth and all the fruit trees for your food. And I have given all the grasses and other green plants to the animals and birds for their food." And so it was. Then God looked over all he had made, and he saw that it was excellent in every way. This

all happened on the sixth day. (Genesis 1:26-31, NLT)

First, please catch the amazing conversation that God has with Himself!! He considers with Himself (the three persons of the Trinity) how He will create man. Listen to Calvin as he comments on this passage:

"Hitherto [in the creation story], God has been introduced simply as commanding; now, when he approaches the most excellent of all his works, he enters into consultation. ...He chose to give this tribute to the excellency of man, that he would, in a manner, enter into consultation concerning his creation. This is the highest honor with which he has dignified us; to a due regard for which, Moses, by this mode of speaking would excite our minds. ...So now, for the purpose of commending to our attention the dignity of our nature, he, in taking counsel concerning the creation of man, testifies that he is about to undertake something great and wonderful. Truly there are many things in this corrupted nature which may induce contempt; but if you rightly weigh all circumstances, man is, among other creatures a certain preeminent specimen of Divine wisdom, justice, and goodness, so that he is deservedly called by the ancients mikri-kosmos, 'a world in miniature.'"

Stop for a moment and let that seep in: the great and honorable thing that separates humans from the animals or any other thing in creation is that we have the distinction of being like our Creator. In the whole story of creation, only here does God stop and consult with Himself concerning the wonderful thing He is about to do. Forgive me, but I must say just a word here about the current position taken by animal rights folks. We human beings are NOT just one more life form upon Spaceship Earth. We are creatures of distinction and glory. We are uniquely crafted and considered by God to be the crown of His creation. We are also unique in our awareness of all of creation and of God.

This is God's favor upon all of mankind. This is grace from the very beginning. This is marvelous beyond our ability to adequately describe or appreciate. Praise Him. Praise Him!

Christians who are no longer sure that God loves and accepts them in Jesus, apart from their present spiritual achievements, are subconsciously radically insecure persons—much less secure than non-Christians, because they have too much light to rest easily under the constant bulletins they receive from their Christian environment about the holiness of God and the righteousness they are supposed to have. Their insecurity shows itself in pride, a fierce defensive assertion of their own righteousness and defensive criticism of others. They come naturally to hate other cultural styles and other races in order to bolster their own security and discharge their suppressed anger. They cling desperately to legal, pharisaical righteousness, but envy, jealousy and other branches on the tree of sin grow out of their fundamental insecurity....It is often necessary to convince sinners (even sinful Christians) of the grace and love of God toward them, before we can get them to look at their problems. Then the vision of grace and the sense of God's forgiving acceptance may actually cure most of the problems. This may account for Paul's frequent fusing of justification and sanctification. ~Richard Lovelace.

Chapter Twenty-Four

Created To Be Aware

Having established our uniqueness in Creation and God's plan, I want to move quickly to the uniqueness of our awareness in our original state before the Fall.

> **The LORD God placed the man in the Garden of Eden to tend and care for it. ...So the LORD God formed from the soil every kind of animal and bird. He brought them to Adam to see what he would call them, and Adam chose a name for each one. He gave names to all the livestock, birds, and wild animals. But still there was no companion suitable for him. (Genesis 2:15, 19-20, NLT)**

God created Adam. He then had all of Creation, the birds and animals "pass" before Adam and he gave him the charge of naming the creatures. However, there was something a little more going on here than just sitting around say-ing, "I think I'll call that one a platypus." This is God's way of showing us that man was created to be aware and at-one with the creation yet also in command over it. In the Hebrew culture, the idea of "naming" something was akin to being in authority over it. When a child is born she is named by the parents. This is both an honor and an indication of the parents' authority over her. Of Genesis 2:19, The Jamison, Fawcett, Brown (JFB) Commentary says concerning Adam naming the creatures,

"His powers of perception and intelligence were super-naturally enlarged to know the characters, habits, and uses of each species that was brought to him."

How's that for awareness!? Not only is man the crown of creation, but he is supernaturally aware of all of the species of Creation! Can you begin to imagine what it would be like to have such a knowledge of your environment and sur-roundings?

Walking with God

Before we leave this passage I must say a word here about the state of awareness between Adam and his God. We see that God Himself brought the animals to Adam. We have no record here (or anywhere else in Eden before the Fall) of Adam finding it difficult to be with God. He is "at home" with God. This is quite astounding, especially in light of the other instances in Scripture where man finds it extremely difficult to behold God and His glory (Isa. 6:1-5; Eze. 1:28; Luke 5:8; Rev. 1:17-18). In our original state we were meant to walk with God and befriend Him as our Father. This, by the way, was one of the shocking things that Jesus preached: God is our Daddy. When asked to teach his disciples to pray, Jesus remarkably replies with, "Our Father…" Amazing. There is a light and wonderful relationship of intimacy with God as we view Adam in the garden. He is aware and he loves it. This is our hearts' cry, isn't it? Don't we long to have this type of relationship with God once again? It is primal. It is in our nature. It is written into our DNA. Mankind scrambles everywhere in search of this intimacy, in search of this lost lover. In Christ, God's love letter to you and me is found. Jesus, the tender, accepting One of love and mercy, is God's hand reaching to us. Let's be bold in seeking this relationship through Christ. Let's drop all this Evangelical mumbo- jumbo of trying to be bigger and better for God. Let's just fall into His merciful arms and say, "I was created for this… Hold me closer Daddy."

Oh, the comfort, the inexpressible comfort of feeling safe with a person: having neither to weigh thoughts nor measure words, but to pour them out. Just as they are—chaff and grain together, knowing that a faithful hand will take and sift them, keep what is worth keeping, and then with the breath of kindness, blow the rest away. ~George Eliot

Chapter Twenty-Five

Humans Created To Be Aware Of Relationships

Having quickly gone over our original awareness of God and the rest of creation, I want us to see how we were created to be aware in our relationships.

> **"At last!" Adam exclaimed. "She is part of my own flesh and bone! She will be called 'woman,' because she was taken out of a man." This explains why a man leaves his father and mother and is joined to his wife, and the two are united into one. Now, although Adam and his wife were both naked, neither of them felt any shame. (Genesis 2:23-25, NLT)**

I really like the way the New Living Translation gives a punch to Adam's statement here. It's like, "Wow!! Shazam!

Look at that!!!" When Adam sees Eve, he exclaims, "At last!" Having reviewed all of creation, Adam still felt a need, an inner yearning for a companion, for completion. It is interesting to note that man yearns for completion outside of himself even when his relationship to God is unmarred. This helps explain our desire, not only for intimacy, but also our yearning for community. More about this later.

Man and woman face one another in total nakedness with no shame. Most commentaries that I have focus on the fact that their lack of shame comes from a lack of sin therefore they had nuttin' to be ashamed of. However, I would like to explore another avenue. This lack of shame is also very indicative of our original state of openness and vulnerability to one another. In our innocence we were made to behold each other wholly, to understand and realize the uniqueness and wonder of one another. As our first parents stood looking at one another without shame, I cannot help but believe that part of that boldness was an understanding of themselves and the other. They had no reason to hide for they had no reason to believe that they would not be loved for who they were. They had an awareness of their need for companionship and community, but this need was not coupled with fear as it is in our lives. The awareness of need was there, especially for Adam but being in a state of "neediness" was not seen as a weakness. How unlike our hearts today.

Needy, needy me

This discussion of NEEDINESS brings me to another point. As creatures (not gods) we have an innate NEED. It is the need for complete exposure through true love and friendship with another person, yet because of the Fall we will never find it completely in this life. Now I can hear some of you say, "Wait, that is what Jesus does. He fulfills that need!" Not true. As pointed out above, both God and Adam recognized that even though they enjoyed an unspoiled relationship, Adam still had a need for the flesh and blood touch of another's care and love. Christ has come to give us a new life; a life that is being restored to a state of unashamedness. This restored life should give us the ability to stand before one another as vulnerable creatures of need; needy for one another.

Our mentor in the faith is Jack Miller. Jack was fond of saying, "Your sins are horrible. You are so bad that you must die. And in Christ, we did die. So you have been ultimately criticized at the Cross. God has judged you to be worthy of Hell. Why then do you still hold onto your reputation and pride as if this judgement were not true."

Or again, Jack would remind people who came to confront him about something that was wrong in his life, "Oh, you think that's bad? If you really knew the truth about me, you would see that it is so much worse." I find it so difficult to emulate this attitude. I would much rather feel "good" about myself and my abilities. I don't want to be reminded that my sins were horrible enough for Christ to die. I don't want to be reminded of my neediness. I want to be strong and in control. Don't we all. Neediness is for losers and geeks.

Neediness paves the way to saltiness

In this upside-down kingdom we have entered, our King once spoke and said,

> **God blesses those who realize their need for him, for the Kingdom of Heaven is given to them.**

> **God blesses those who mourn, for they will be comforted.**

> *God blesses those who are gentle and lowly, for the whole earth will belong to them.*
>
> *God blesses those who are hungry and thirsty for justice, for they will receive it in full.*
>
> *God blesses those who are merciful, for they will be shown mercy.*
>
> *God blesses those whose hearts are pure, for they will see God.*
>
> *God blesses those who work for peace, for they will be called the children of God.*
>
> *God blesses those who are persecuted because they live for God, for the Kingdom of Heaven is theirs. (Matthew 5:3-10, NLT)*

Why? What is so great about all these weird things that God finds so attractive? Needy, poor, mourning, persecuted… yuk, sounds like a chick flick gone bad. I believe that one of the main points the King is making here is: awareness. Blessed are you, Charlie, when you begin to be aware of your deep need and are vulnerable enough to stand "naked" before others. Blessed are you when you see your needs, hurts and pains for you are in a much better place to see these things in others and help them as well. Blessed are you when you stop trying to be something you were not created to be. Blessed are you when you are real and NOT religious. It is then that you begin to be the Salt, the preservative in your household and in your community.

Let us pray to the King that we might be restored to our original state of unashamed neediness. Let us, today, go into the world with an awareness of our nakedness. We might be surprised at what happens.

We are never nearer Christ than when we find ourselves lost in a holy amazement at His unspeakable love. ~John Owen

Chapter Twenty-Six

Awareness Is Bliss

Having now established a few things about our original state, let's review. We were created to be aware of God and His adoration of us. We were created to be aware of the created world and to have a vice-regent's hand in cultivating it as well as having authority over it. We were created to be aware of our intimate allies (spouses) as well as other humans. Our awareness was that virtue (of sorts) which made us fully human; fully aware of God, of man, of beast and universe. When I say "fully" I mean our awareness was as full as a creature could have. As mentioned earlier, we are not gods. We are creatures of God, made in His image. We had God-like awareness, but not God's awareness; yet our unspoiled awareness of Him and His creation made us fully human, fully alive.

So what's the scoop with all this awareness junk?

I wanted to review what we have covered so far and state my original premise: for most of our lives here on earth we are quite unaware of God and His movement in our lives and if you are sort of a "religious" type or part of the Evangelical ghetto, like me, it is my contention that we are probably the most unaware (but this will be covered later). Most of my dealings with God have come in fits and starts of yelling, sinfulness, selfishness, arrogance, cursing, anger and rage which eventually give way to an awareness of His love for me. But, even in my saner moments, I remain basically Unaware of Him. Alas, we see through a glass darkly. Yet in spite of it all, there is grace for the unaware!

Ease up!!

Let me share a story (from memory) with you that I once heard from Dudley Hall. Dudley is a wonderful minister of the Gospel and you can find out more about his ministry at http://www.sclm.org/. Dudley was exchanging greetings with a Christian friend, when the friend said, "Dudley, what's up with you. You just seem so peaceful. It's like you have learned how to sit down on the inside. How do you do that?" Dudley thought for a moment and said, "Well, I don't know… I guess I have my moments of fear, panic and anger like anyone else and I have always had one of those 'Type A' personalities. But I suppose what you detect in me… Well, I guess you see in me… Let me put it like this: there was a time when I was praying and I saw God. I don't mean I had some great vision or physical manifestation, I mean, I caught a glimpse–just a glimpse of the immensity and wonder of God [awareness] and I suppose it changed me. You see, I believe that when we get to heaven, we'll praise Him and worship Him and all that but before any of that commences, I believe we're gonna get up there, look around, see Him and His care for us on this earth and we're gonna slap ourselves on the forehead and shout, 'Good Golly Miss Molly!! If I had known He was THIS much in control… I would've eased up a long time ago!!'"

This, my friends, is one of the few honest responses we should have when we become aware of God and the immensity of His love for us in Christ. As a matter of fact, I wouldn't be surprised if when we get to Heaven, we find all the saints who have gone there before us with red and bruised foreheads!! That's what I hope to have fully developed here in this life before I go to Heaven: a red forehead from slapping myself whenever I am astounded at Him and my heretofore unawareness of Him. "Good Golly, if I had only known, how close He was during my heartache." "If I had only known how wonderfully things would turn out." "If I had only known how many blessings He placed all around me to keep me sane," etc… etc… etc.

Yes, I hope–no, I pray that together we will become more aware of, and thus more thankful for, all that He is and has done. And as this happens, we learn to trust.

Sin is the dare of God's justice, the rape of His mercy, the jeer of His patience, the slight of His power, and the contempt of His love. ~John Bunyan

Chapter Twenty-Seven

The Lust To BE God

In our created state, we were made to be aware of God, His creation and our environment. If we had left it like this, all would be right with the world. However, it has been human nature (even from the very beginning) to LUST for more than we have, even if what we have is PERFECT. Quite amazing, huh? God made the whole world for our delight and in all the universe he pastes up just one little "Wet Paint – Do Not Touch" sign. And what do we do? We run with all our might to touch the darn thing!!! People are funny. Or is it, people are tragic? I suppose it is both; we laugh 'til we cry and cry 'til we laugh.

You're killing me with RULES...
er... I mean... OK, OK... maybe it's just
ONE rule but it still bugs me!

As Adam and Eve enjoyed the Creation and one another, they came upon a tempter in the form of a serpent. This serpent put within the heart of Eve the need for that ONE thing she did not possess: the same awareness that God has. Let's look at the passage:

> *Now the serpent was the shrewdest of all the creatures the LORD God had made. "Really?" he asked the woman. "Did God really say you must not eat any of the fruit in the garden?" "Of course we may eat it," the woman told him. "It's only the fruit from the tree at the center of the garden that we are not allowed to eat. God says we must not eat it or even touch it, or we will die." "You won't die!" the serpent hissed. "God knows that your eyes will be opened when you eat it. You will become just like God, knowing everything, both good and evil." (Genesis 3:1-5, NLT)*

I will not exposit this passage because I would do such a poor job and I do not consider myself a theologian or a preacher. (There are chefs and there are those who heat-up pork & beans. I am the latter.) That having been said I would like to point out Satan's immediate plan of attack, "That mean, old God! Can you believe what He said?? He said you can't eat from ANY tree in the garden!! I am outraged; aren't you?" A rebellious heart and a rebellious nature takes any law or rule and exaggerates it a hundred times out of proportion! Just look at what happens when folks try to get decency laws passed or when people try to stem the tide of horror and debasement in our music and movies; what's the first thing we hear? "You are trying to stamp out ALL our freedoms! If we listened to you we would have book burnings and public hangings and people spying in our homes to make certain we were following ALL your confining rules!! You want to control our WHOLE LIVES!" Sound familiar? The flesh is very susceptible to this type of temptation and if you are still not convinced, then I suggest you listen to any child in the range of two to twenty-one years of age talk to their parents, "You NEVER let me do ANYTHING!!" or "You're ALWAYS saying NO to EVERYTHING I want to do!!" It was this rebellion that Satan had in his own nature and that he tried to thrust upon Eve.

The birth of legalism

It is interesting to note that Eve is able to stand up to the outrage of Satan and his attack. But then she does a strange thing. Eve quotes the command of God back to Satan but adds a little extra dressing. She adds the phrase, "...or even touch it." This was not in the original command. This was a little something extra she threw in to sort of make the command "stick" better. God didn't say they couldn't touch the fruit. As far we know, they could have picked one of those fruits and used it as a baseball or as a nice centerpiece for the dinner table. But as is human nature, Eve begins her own little Talmud, her own little legalism to make certain they didn't eat of the fruit. She sort of re-words the sign, "Wet Paint – Do Not Touch... AND Don't Even Think About Looking At This Wall Until The Paint Is Dry – Stay 100 yards away!" This tendency has been in the heart of every person who has ever thought about following God's word; the pull towards legalism. It was in our original parents and it remains in most of us "religious" folks today.

Let me tell you a little story, amongst thousands, about how I have seen this tendency flesh itself out. I spent a few years in a fundamentalist church while in high school. The pastor was telling the congregation one Sunday night about the new associate pastor who was to arrive within the month. The pastor said, "You think I've got convictions. This man has convictions I never even thought of!!" For those of you who are not "hip" to Evan/Fundy lingo, a "conviction" is primarily something that you WILL NOT do, WILL NOT associate with or WILL NOT condone in others when you see them doing it. It is these "convictions" that give Evangelicals such a great name in the United States and other places where legalism reigns.

Anyway, back to the story. Sure enough, when the associate pastor arrived, one of the first sermons he preached admonished us that Christian people should not buy pretzels! You heard me, I said "pretzels." Why? Well, because pretzels were associated with beer and if people saw you buying pretzels they had a reasonable right to think that you had some beer hiding somewhere. Good Golly! Can you see how the prescription not to get drunk, went from there to "no drinking," to not being anywhere where alcohol was served, to not buying pretzels? Of course, there are hundreds of really cool legalistic rules I just glossed over in that last sentence. The "logical" progression from the Biblical prescription of no drunkenness to not buying pretzels is actually much, much longer with all sorts of "cool" contusions of Scripture to justify a point.

Just ease up!

I want to remind you once again that my heart's tendency and your heart's tendency is to constantly make this "God-thing" much more complex than it really is. It is seen in our original parents. It is seen as we become so weird and anal-retentive with ourselves that our lives become lifeless and antiseptic as we seek not only to "not eat the fruit" but also to "not even touch it." What rules and strange habits have you added to your own life and conscience that you think you MUST perform in order to gain more of God's love? Does it sound something like this, "Not only must I pray, but I also must have my eyes closed and head bowed and really, really concentrate really hard so God will know how serious I am. These are the only REAL prayers that God pays attention to." Or does it sound like this, "I know that God loves me in Christ, but if I act really, really holy and I don't laugh at the wrong jokes or don't get too angry (in public) or never raise my voice, then He will love me more and I'll get the added bonus of other people knowing how holy I am."

Well, ease up my friend. Ease up and enjoy the wonder of all that God has placed before you. Get back to the basics, as Jesus told His disciples, "But don't rejoice just because evil spirits obey you; rejoice because your names are registered as citizens of heaven." (Luke 10:20, NLT) This is an amazing statement! The disciples were coming to tell Him that such power had descended upon them and their ministry that even the demons were obeying them!!! Jesus said, "That's not a big deal. The REALLY big deal is that the Father loves you and has written your name in a very special book, His book of Loved Ones whom He wants to spend Eternity with." Cool. Very Cool. Ease up, fellow citizen.

Chapter Twenty-Eight

The Deed Is Done And Doom Descends

We have been building a foundation for the assertion: There is grace for the unaware. In even the most holy saint who ever lived, there is a lack of awareness of God and His true nature towards us. However, before examining our unawareness I have attempted to show that we were originally created to be aware of Him, the creation and our fellow humans. We have been looking at the man and woman in Eden.

Moving from Satan's first line of temptation of trying to twist God's command into some strange philosophical pretzel and Eve's somewhat brave come back, we now move to Satan's "Plan B" in tempting our parents:

> *"Of course we may eat it," the woman told him. "It's only the fruit from the tree at the center of the garden that we are not allowed to eat. God says we must not eat it or even touch it, or we will die." "You won't die!" the serpent hissed. "God knows that*

*your eyes will be opened when you eat it. You will become just
like God, knowing everything, both good and evil." The woman
was convinced. The fruit looked so fresh and delicious, and it
would make her so wise! So she ate some of the fruit. She also
gave some to her husband, who was with her. Then he ate it,
too. (Genesis 3:2-6, NLT)*

Yo, yo, yo...
you be God, Momma!

Here Satan jumps in with both feet… er… uh… scales or
something like that. He pounces upon God's Word and
immediately questions its veracity. "God is a liar!" the
tempter hisses out with all the hatred and venom he can
muster. He then sort of composes himself and explains, "Ok,
look at it this way: God, that paranoid fool, is just afraid that
you will become as aware as He is. Just look at yourself, you
are like God in every other way. OK, maybe you're not
omnipresent and maybe you can't create *ex nihilo* (from nothing) and perhaps just a few other little things, but basically
you are like God in every way except you don't have His
awareness. He is keeping some really neat stuff to Himself
and He won't let you have it!"

Before proceeding I would like to stop here and point out
another common heresy concerning God and His providence
over our lives. We are constantly being tempted to believe
that God is withholding something from us. If He would just
stop teasing us and let us have all that we need and want,
THEN we could really live a great life… why, we could even
be great witnesses!! This temptation is our constant companion through life. And guess what, Christians are the suckers
of the universe when it comes to falling for this one! Having
tasted of God's love and care, we are shocked to one day
find that all is not going as we think it should. "Hey, what
gives here, God? Look, I understand you must have a very
limited perspective on this whole issue and that's why I am
telling you–Hey, wait a minute! You don't have a limited

perspective, you're in charge of everything. So if You are in charge of everything and I am still so very miserable… then You are purposely keeping something back from me that would make me complete and happy!" Sound familiar? Maybe you don't use these very same words, but it is a common pothole we trip into. At the core of our unhappiness, fears and doubts is this unspoken whisper, "God is holding back." This was the center of Satan's Plan B, and it worked so well he has used it as Plan A ever since.

The sin came before the act

It is at this point that Eve, who has had her defenses worn down to a nub, commits the sin which sends humankind down the drain of dreariness and deep, dank darkness. The real sin was not the taking of the fruit and eating, although that was a sin. The REAL sin of Eve was her sudden assertion of autonomy from God. In the New Living Translation quoted above, it says, "the woman was convinced." This tends to gloss over a rather dramatic scene painted for us in the NIV and other versions:

> *When the woman saw that the fruit of the tree was good for food and pleasing to the eye, and also desirable for gaining wisdom, she took some and ate it. She also gave some to her husband, who was with her, and he ate it. (Genesis 3:6, NIV)*

Here, we sort of see the wheels turning in Eve's head. She looks at the fruit and considers the benefits. She sees that it is nice to look at and that it even looks like it might make her wise if she took a bite. Here we have THE SIN. Van Til has pointed out that this was the real sin of Eve and continues to be THE SIN of every person since. You see, it is at this point that Eve makes an independent stand apart from God and says to herself, "On one hand, I have God and His word; on the other hand, I have the Snake and his word. But guess what? I am wiser than either one of those guys and I have the ability to decide for myself what is best!" It is here that we witness Eve turning to the tree and beginning to consider the situation; doing her own little scientific analysis. Rather than relying upon and acknowledging the Word of her Creator, the creature exhibits a rebellious independence and says, "I am the final arbiter of reality! I am able to distinguish and discern all things important in my life! I am the captain of my own boat!" Can you begin to see what a silly position this is? A creature "on the scene" for just a short time suddenly begins to think she has more brains than her Creator. For a great treatment of this subject and its relation to defending the faith, see Richard Pratt's book, *Every Thought Captive*.

Grabbing the golden ring of awareness

Eve "stands tall" and asserts herself as the ultimate interpreter of reality, the final and fixed reference point of her life. On the basis of her own independence from God, she takes the fruit and eats it. But why does she eat it? She wants more awareness! She wants the extra special thing that will make her equal with God. She wants this "secret" knowledge that will set her apart from all else. So here we have this weirdness: man was created to be the most aware of any creature but as he grabs for more awareness, he becomes unaware. I told you it was weird. Our awareness was given by God for love, life, happiness, wisdom, tenderness and intimacy to name but a few of the benefits. Yet this awareness when used for autonomy and selfishness becomes blindness and death.

What are the ways we have taken the awareness God has given us and turned it into arrogance and autonomy? Not sure what I am asking? Let's try this one. Have you ever read something about Him or learned something from Him and your first thought is how to tell others about it so they can see how spiritual you are? Or perhaps your awareness extends to a passage in the Bible and one of your first thoughts is how much _____ (insert name of friend or family member here) needs to hear this!! How often have we used the revelations of God as extra ammunition to unload on an unsuspecting world? Have you ever memorized some Scripture with one of your primary motivators being how wise you will appear in front of others? These are just a few ways that we take the awareness of God and immediately turn it into blindness and faithlessness.

But take heart, fellow citizen. I have heard a proclamation in the town square, the King has turned a bit weird and He has fallen in love with blind, faithless people. The story continues...

Whatsoever is good for God's children they shall have it; for all is theirs to help them towards heaven; therefore if poverty be good they shall have it; if disgrace or crosses be good they shall have them; for all is ours to promote our greatest prosperity. ~Richard Sibbes

Chapter Twenty-Nine

Our Lust For The Secret

In the heart of every person we find a strange craving for something more. The grass, it seems, has always been greener on the other side. Contentment has never been a virtue we exercise very well. We see Satan catering to this quirky desire for something more in the temptation of Eve. As mentioned earlier, this desire springs from the belief that God is holding back. He is keeping the really neat stuff for Himself. But even more telling than that; we have a core conviction that we DESERVE something more. We deserve all the rights, knowledge (awareness), and attributes of God.

Spank that baby! Please!!

It is difficult for us, as fallen creatures, to see the absurdity of this assertion–that we deserve more from God. But let me try an analogy. Imagine that you have given birth to a baby who can talk within a few hours of delivery. You bring your bundle of joy home and place him in his crib. The baby spends a few minutes looking around and then announces, "Thanks for the crib, toys, bedroom and such, but you're not really giving me everything that will make me a complete, self-actualized baby." (This kid has a great vocabulary!!) The baby stands up in the crib and not only demands that you give him more than what he's got, but he also accuses you of holding back some very important information about the household. He chastises you, "I see you have a great kitchen in there, but you haven't even told me where to find the Sugar Smacks! And that TV in the next room, you didn't show me how to use the remote, did ya, huh? Listen, if I am gonna live in this place, you better start letting me in on some of this secret knowledge. I have just as much right as you do to have all the household knowledge and the secret passwords to the AOL account. And, oh, by the way, I need you to feed me, clothe me, take total care of me and, uh… I just made a mess in my diaper; you should change me real soon."

After calling the hospital to make certain there wasn't some mistake and you (hopefully) brought home the wrong baby, you sit down and find that you are disappointed and hurt. There is nothing… NOTHING which you are withholding from your child. The food, the room, the toys, everything is geared to give your baby a wonderful life. All the things he is complaining about you will one day teach him and bring him up-to-speed on. In your wisdom, you know that a kid who messes in his diapers does not have the full capabilities of an adult. You know how to raise a child and you know that children are not capable of taking in everything at once. But even further than that, you realize that you are the parent in this relationship and all things are not equal… and never will be. You are the "creator" of this child and the natural order of things dictates the creature will always be subservient to the creator. Creatures do not auto-matically DESERVE to be equal with their creators.

Let me go! Let me fall!!

Leaving the baby locked away in an all-steel crib with tamper-proof locks, we turn our attention to our hearts and our tendencies to act just like Baby Brat above. In the heart of our original mother, we find this same attitude arising as she gives way to temptation and takes her "independent" stand from God. Eve became Baby Brat and accused God of not letting go of the really good stuff. There was so much God was not telling her. There were so many ways God was keeping her from becoming a vital, self-actualized woman (hear her roar). Well, guess what, this is the state of my heart and your heart. Confounded by life–the twists and turns of Providence–our first reaction is, quite often, to shake our fists at God and say, "You have not given me enough for life and fulfillment! You are keeping back the really good stuff that would make me a happy person! And if you won't give it to me, I have decided to get it myself. And oh, by the way, I still need You to take care of me and continue to give me all the other really amazing blessings you have given me (change my diaper), so that I can continue my rebellion against you."

Van Til has remarked that unregenerate man is like a child who is being held in a parent's arms which are protect-ing him from falling into a deep flaming pit. Yet the whole time the child is being protected in the parent's arms, he is hitting and slapping the parent about the face.

This is, all too often, a picture of me and my reaction to Providence. How about you? Is God really holding back the good stuff from you so He can enjoy watching you be miser-able? Has He really not given you the things you need for life, love and happiness? Is there really that secret truth "out there" somewhere that will cause everything to "click" in your life once you discover it? Do you think you might find it–the secret–in the next weekend seminar? Perhaps on that evangelical cruise vacation, you will stumble upon that spiritual secret which will allow you to rise above it all and never struggle again.

P-ç-ç-ç-t! Wanna know a secret?

Ruth has taught me a hymn she learned as a child. I don't even know the title of it. We have always called it 444 in the Trinity Hymnal. It is a hymn of submission and honor to our Creator. It is a hymn of acceptance; accepting God's providence and lordship in our lives. We sing this hymn quite often in the car together but most often when times are difficult for us. Let me quote a few verses:

Father, I know that all my life
is portioned out for me,
The changes that are sure to come,
I do not fear to see.
I ask thee for a present mind,
intent on pleasing Thee.

I would not have the restless will
that hurries to and fro,
Seeking for some great thing to do
or secret thing to know.
I would be treated as a child
and guided where I go.

There is more to this hymn but please read that second verse once more. It is the restless will that hurries after the GREAT thing. We are somewhat trapped in a culture where fame and greatness are synonymous with blessing and happiness.

• We don't want to start a business, we want to start A MULTI-MILLION DOLLAR, MULTI-NATIONAL ORGANI-ZATION!!!!!

• We don't want to have a ministry, we want a FAMOUS, SIGNIFICANT, MASS MARKET APPEAL MINISTRY, where we can get all the perks of fame and fortune and yet look spiritual at the same time!

• We don't want to be a pastor; we want TO RULE OVER A GROWING, THRIVING CHURCH OF THOUSANDS, complete with parking lot attendants, food court and a twenty million dollar budget.

Now look at the other red flag of a restless will: a quest for the secret thing to know. Why is this a sign of a restless will? The restless will is not convinced that "this" is enough. There must be something more out there that I am missing. Life must be easier than this. There must be a key that God has not given me yet which will open up the mysteries of life and allow me to have peace.

Go to a Christian bookstore... aw, heck... go to ANY bookstore and the vast majority of the books and titles appeal to this inherent weakness in our nature: the quest for the Secret. The Secret of Life. Just the word "secret" causes my heart to beat a little faster and my eyes to open a bit wider. To know a secret... THE secret... how cool would that be??

So what's THE secret? The one word answer is as profound as it is confusing (and a bit disappointing): Jesus. That's it. Nothing more. At one point in Jesus' ministry, a bunch of people who had been following Him turned away, convinced that Jesus did NOT have THE secret. As the crowd was walking away, Jesus turned to the twelve disciples and asked, "You leaving too?" Peter responds, "Where would we go? You have the Words of Eternal Life. You,

Lord, are THE secret." Forgive my gross paraphrasing but I do believe that Peter was saying something like this, "No, Jesus. We have learned NOT to have a restless will. We have found THE secret and it is to ease up and relax in the fact that you are IT."

Chapter Thirty

The Sin Of Adam And Loss Of Awareness

Having trounced on Eve's head for the past several chapters, we turn our attention to Adam. Let's look at the text first.

> **The woman was convinced. The fruit looked so fresh and delicious, and it would make her so wise! So she ate some of the fruit. She also gave some to her husband, who was with her. Then he ate it, too. At that moment, their eyes were opened, and they suddenly felt shame at their nakedness. So they strung fig leaves together around their hips to cover themselves. Toward evening they heard the LORD God walking about in the garden, so they hid themselves among the trees. (Genesis 3:6-8, NLT)**

Wow, what a guy! OK, let's get this picture in our minds. Adam and Eve are out for a stroll. Perhaps they are out to visit the lions or maybe they want to walk the badger. But for some reason Eve gets wrapped-up in a deep conversation with THE snake. Now according to the passage, Adam was right there with Eve the whole dang time. We might be tempted to make some excuses for Adam. You know, he might have found the first remote control ever created lying on the ground and he suddenly starts flipping through channels faster than Eve could retain his interest. Or maybe Adam begins to wonder why he doesn't have a belly button and is navel-gazing. But the plain truth is Adam was just watching and observing this conversation!! Amazing! Even from the beginning, men had a hard time with conversation! That's probably why Eve started talking to the snake. Adam was just no good at sharing his thoughts; unlike most men since that time, who love to engage in long conversations about their feelings and how their day went at work!

No kidding, what do you think was going on in Adam's mind? How could he just stand by and watch his wife be deceived and fall into sin? May I suggest that just as Eve committed her sin before she ever took the fruit, so also, Adam committed his sin before the fruit was given to him by his wife. Adam was placed in the garden to be a leader and cultivate his environment. He was to co-reign with God over paradise! But here we find Adam too tired or too lazy or too scared to take his responsibility seriously. He stands by and abdicates his role of leader. How sad. This was the beginning of Adam's sin.

Taking a quick detour from the passage, the verse that I immediately think of when I read Genesis 3 is Paul's strange statement (read: monkey wrench) when speaking to Timothy:

> *And it was the woman, not Adam, who was deceived by Satan, and sin was the result. (1 Timothy 2:14, NLT)*

Interesting. The woman was deceived and sinned, yet it is obvious that Adam sinned as well. But Paul's point here seems to be that Eve had her mind twisted; Adam did not; therefore one is left with the impression that Adam wasn't deceived. He just barreled head long into sin knowing he was sinning! Read the context. By the way, I don't see how being deceived is any worse than just shrugging your shoulders and saying, "What the heck… Might as well break the Covenant with God today." But that whole line of thought is for another time and a whole 'nother subject: women in the church. Yikes!!!

From independence to cowardice and apathy

In Romans 5 Paul makes it clear that by Adam's sin, all sinned. So Adam's fall into sin and rebellion was no small thing. But what was his sin? We have covered the issues involved in Eve's sin, but what about the guy? Eve took a bold step to proclaim her independence from God and His Word, but it would appear from the passage that at the core of Adam's sin was cowardice and negligence. Is cowardice a sin? Darn tootin'. Cowardice denies God's statement of reality. What about the spies who went with Joshua to the Promised Land. They wilted with fear and trembling. What about the disciples afraid when the storm rises? God's statements of reality in these instances indicated that God would triumph in and through these circumstances but the sin of Cowardice says, "No, you're wrong. I am afraid because you obviously don't know what's really going on here." I think there was a bit of FEAR going on in Adam's sin. I think he was afraid to assert himself as rightful "lord." He was afraid, as most of us are when witnessing, that he wouldn't have all the answers. Sound familiar?

Understanding our innate shortcomings

It is sad to see our first father acting so niggardly. (By the way, not a racist word. Look it up.) But by understanding Adam's sin, we, as men, can begin to understand ourselves and the damage we do in our relationships. For whatever reason, Adam has decided that he has had a rough day and he isn't about to waste time and energy getting involved in his wife's world. He was detached and "watchin' TV." This was the first step of separation from both his rightful place as "lord" of creation and as husband to his wife. In a movie or play, isn't it sad when we observe that instant when the protagonist does something–perhaps makes a small, "insignificant" decision that sends the course of his life into disarray? Here it is, that sad moment when Adam decides to retreat and become uninvolved.

Dear brothers, or to put it another way, Yo guys, how many times has this happened in our own lives this past week? This sin is so common to the married man that it takes God's Spirit to truly allow us to see and recognize it.

I want us to just sort of simmer here for a while. But do simmer. Please simmer. Look at your attitude when coming home from work. Do you notice your spouse and what she is doing? Do you creatively enter into her world? Do you engage in the "conversations" she is having in her reality? Ask God to show you the ways that you have been like Adam in the very conception of his first sin against God. We husbands have been given the role of "lord" over our households, yet don't we behave just like Adam in this scene? Don't we withdraw and sort of hope everything works out for the better, knowing that it won't, but we're just too tired to "deal with anything" right now? Do you understand how cruel and horrible this can be? Adam did not and we, today, do not. We need God to come and show us our sin for what it is and then run to Him for forgiveness. Let's do that, OK?

The worst is always very near the best; there is something much worse than Atheism which is Satanism; otherwise known as Being God. ~G.K. Chesterton

Chapter Thirty-One

Men Just Gots To Be Right!

I would like to continue my treatment of the Fall of humankind. But I would like to inform those of you who skipped ahead to this chapter because of its title (men) what our goal is in these pages of the last chapters. It is my contention that grace comes to us in thousands of ways and covers thousands of sins. However, in my life I have found that these sins can be categorized in three different areas: unawareness, ingratitude and unspirituality. We have been dealing with the first area: how unaware we are of God and His love toward us and yet how our unawareness will not keep us from Christ's love; He covers that as well. We are continuing our look at how we lost our awareness of God and the implications there of. Let's get started.

Aw, Adam... you scaredy cat!

Adam, as we discovered in the previous chapter, was with Eve when she was deceived by Satan. He was there and observed the whole thing. Let's look at the NIV:

> *Now the serpent was more crafty than any of the wild animals the LORD God had made. He said to the woman, "Did God really say, 'You must not eat from any tree in the garden?'" The woman said to the serpent, "We may eat fruit from the trees in the garden, but God did say, 'You must not eat fruit from the tree that is in the middle of the garden, and you must not touch it, or you will die.'" "You will not surely die," the serpent said to the woman. "For God knows that when you eat of it your eyes will be opened, and you will be like God, knowing good and evil." When the woman saw that the fruit of the tree was good for food and pleasing to the eye, and also desirable for gaining wisdom, she took some and ate it. She also gave some to her husband, who was with her, and he ate it. (Genesis 3:1-6, NIV)*

Read it and weep! Eve gave some to her husband, who was with her! We have already talked about Adam's abdication of leadership through lack of involvement, so I would now like to focus on Adam's fear regarding getting involved with his wife and her world. It is my speculation, or should I say, my deduction from the rest of Scripture, that Adam's lack of leadership springs from a fear of not knowing what to do or how to handle the situation.

Through all the Scriptures of both the Old and New Testaments we see this pattern of God's command going out and man's natural reaction of fear in confronting that command. Moses' reaction to God's call was one of argument and distrust concerning God's intelligence in choosing him to lead Israel. Gideon feared his call from God and kept stacking up all kinds of tests for God to pass in order to convince him that God was not insane. The prophets complained and trembled at their task of proclaiming God's word to hostile audiences. The Apostles quaked with doubt and unbelief over and over again as they were sent out into the world with God's command. I believe that this is part of the problem with Adam when he comes to a crossroads in his mandate from God to be "lord" over all creation.

Before venturing further, let me ask you a question. What causes you to hesitate and not proceed forward in a matter? Is it not that you are afraid your words or actions may not be the appropriate ones? Have you ever known what you should do but just were not sure of the outcome so you did nothing? Is this not fear?

Called to be right?

Adam's entanglement in sin was made all the more complex by his silence when he should have shown leadership. But I am wondering if Adam did not have the (now) typical man's reaction to the situation of thinking that God had not called him to be faithful, but rather he was convinced that God had called him to be RIGHT. This is more responsibility than most of us can handle. I do believe that men are an angry bunch o' people for this very reason: they think they should be RIGHT in every circumstance and if not RIGHT then at least they should know how to handle a situation. As a man, my first reaction to someone complaining of a problem or stressful situation in their life is to pronounce the RIGHT answer OR suggest THE remedy for what they should do or how they should act. We're men–we want to fix it! That's what we are supposed to do. We gotta fix it! We want to fix everything. We want to make it right. And when things don't go right or if our commands are not followed, then we "hit the ceiling" with frustration and anger.

Getting back to Adam and his silence. Well, put yourself in Adam's shoes... er... feet. This was possibly the first threat to his world-life view. This snake comes along and starts spouting some mumbo--jumbo to his wife and I think he freezes in fear. He did not know exactly how to answer.

He did not know how to BE right in this situation. Therefore, he let it pass. Woefully, he let it pass.

I confess to appreciating and listening to Dr. Laura Schlesinger. And every now and then she gets calls from people asking about a moral dilemma with their kids. Dr. Laura will respond with, "Tom, do you think your grandparents would have agonized over this?" The caller will respond with, "No." And Dr. Laura will say, "That's right. They had a code of ethics and morals and they would let everyone know about it no matter whether they looked too rigid or not. They proceeded with life, not caring if their kids thought they were insensitive!" And this, I believe is at the root of the era of permissiveness we see in our society. Too many people, following Adam's lead, hang back, afraid that they will not do or say the right thing (especially not the right thing that will make them popular, "hip" and "with it") therefore, nothing gets said.

This, by the way, brings up another pet subject of mine: the "christian" personality and how disgusting it is!! In the Evangelical world we have developed a "christian" way of acting, talking and reacting to things which will always "look" right, but in actuality is nothing more than a fear of not looking spiritual or not following the rules of this little sub-culture!! But that is for another book.

So as we look at Adam and see his sin, what is it that we see reflected back in us? Is it not that we feel like we should "have our act together" before we take leadership or even comment on certain circumstances? I am not talking about making ourselves obnoxious by always feeling like our opinion should be spouted out whenever there is a lull in the conversation. But I am talking about speaking the truth in every situation. Imagine if Adam had just spoken the truth to his wife and to the snake. He didn't have to say it just RIGHT; he just had to be faithful. Something to think about.

When God calls a man, He does not repent of it. God does not, as many friends do, love one day and hate another, or as princes, who make their subjects favorites, and afterwards throw them into prison. This is the blessedness of a saint; his condition admits of no alteration. God's call is founded on His decree, and His decree is immutable. Acts of grace cannot be reversed. God blots out His people's sins, but not their names. ~Thomas Watson

Chapter Thirty-Two

God's Favor To The Unaware

Although he had been created to be aware of God and His wonder, man chose instead to look for something more. He chose to abdicate, to run, to hide, to side-step… in short, he chose to sin.

We have discovered that man, in his original state, had a view of and a relationship with God and his environment that we are unable to even imagine. God and man talked openly with one another. There was no fear, no wall of separation between them. Man, imitating His Father, was given the honor of speaking words into his environment to "make it so" as he names the animals. Man was given the whole earth as his garden and he was to reign with God over the whole of creation. Man was then given a companion, the

Woman, who was taken from his side, whom he was to protect and love. At the Fall, all this changed. All changed forever and we all groan to be made whole once again.

Lost: our awareness of God

When man fell, God promised Adam that he would die and he did. I sometimes wish that he had died immediately rather than passing this bad seed of sin onto his progeny. But physically, he did not die immediately. No he lived his life as a sinner, with another sinner and gave birth to other sinners. However, there was an immediate death in man's sin. It was the death of soul; the death of true common sense; the death of awareness. It was as if a huge foggy cloud descended over man's being and he could not reason with or see anything beyond the tip of his nose. The view he had of God and creation was suddenly obscured by the death shroud of sin and rebellion. In short, man became a dolt! Now lest we misunderstand, when I write "man" I am referring to humankind, men AND women. There is more than just one gender condemned to dolt-hood! Hey, maybe that is where we get the word, "adulthood."

If you've made it this far in the book then you know how inept man has become in matters related to God and spirituality. He lost his awareness and thus his ability to comprehend how he fits into the universe. With God and His word obscured, man wanders and becomes truly lost in a world which only gets curiouser and curiouser! It is this type of foggy-headed, cloud-shrouded human that the angels find so difficult to understand.

Angels, by the way, say the strangest things to humans. At the empty tomb, they ask, "Why seek the living among the dead?" Or with the shepherds they float down out of the sky like a bad dream about UFOs and say, 'Don't be afraid."

But the angels have spiritual vision and I can't help but think that they are pretty amazed at our spiritual blindness. Even those of us who are of faith!

Awareness gone... God obscured

As Adam and Eve's sin plunged them into death, both spiritual and physical, they lost the ability to see and talk to God as they once had. Meditate with me and think upon the ways our own vision of God has been obscured. Let me just list some ways we Christians have mis-characterized our Father. Now keep in mind, these statements are not ideas that we would openly verbalize. We're far too "spiritual" for that, but nonetheless, we have these very revealing, sub-conscious thoughts:

- God is mean and must be appeased by my works and obedience.

- God waits for me to make a mistake, then he delights in punishing me.

- God is unconcerned about the problems in my life because I have been so bad. He's ignoring me and I deserve to be ignored.

- God is an old man with little patience with me.

- God is cold and retreating. He likes watching me suffer while He remains silent.

- God doesn't really care about my circumstances. If he did He would treat me differently.

- God cannot really be satisfied with only faith. I must DO more and BE more.

- Good things, things that I really enjoy, don't really come from God. He doesn't really want me to have THAT much fun.

- God won't hear my prayers if I haven't had my devotions regularly.

Do any of these things sound familiar? If not to your head, then to your heart? Perhaps my proclivities are different than most but I find myself constantly tempted in these ways.

This is where I must cry out to His Spirit and ask Him to teach my weary heart about Jesus. This is faith in it's finest hour. "Blessed are the poor in spirit..." When we recognize our poverty then we can turn to the riches of Christ.

Speaking of poverty and riches, this seems to be a recurring theme throughout the New Testament. It is only those who see their poverty who have the inkling to seek out riches they do not have. It is only those who see their weakness who seek strength and refuge in Another. It is only those who have lost their lives who find it the eyes and heart of Another.

So turn! Face boldly your sins of presumption and accusation towards our Father God. Confess and repent of your unbelieving heart, then God will come like a warrior king to save and rescue.

Does this mean He will eliminate all difficulties from you life? No. But it does mean you will receive the wisdom and strength to endure such hardships with supernatural resilience.

God's favor to the unspiritual, unappreciative and unaware. Amen.

IF YOU ARE A PREACHER OF MERCY, do not preach an imaginary but the true mercy. If the mercy is true, you must therefore bear the true, not an imaginary sin. God does not save those who are only imaginary sinners. Be a sinner, and let your sins be strong, but let your trust in Christ be stronger, and rejoice in Christ who is the victor over sin, death, and the world. We will commit sins while we are here, for this life is not a place where justice resides. We, however, says Peter (2. Peter 3:13) are looking forward to a new heaven and a new earth where justice will reign. It suffices that through God's glory we have recognized the Lamb who takes away the sin of the world. No sin can separate us from Him, even if we were to kill or commit adultery thousands of times each day. Do you think such an exalted Lamb paid merely a small price with a meager sacrifice for our sins? Pray hard for you are quite a sinner. ~~ MARTIN LUTHER

"THE FATUOUS IDEA THAT A PERSON CAN BE HOLY by himself denies God the pleasure of saving sinners. God must therefore first take the sledge-hammer of the Law in His fists and smash the beast of self-righteousness and its brood of self-confidence, self-wisdom, self-righteousness, and self-help. When the conscience has been thoroughly frightened by the Law it welcomes the Gospel of grace with its message of a Savior Who came…not to break the bruised reed, nor to quench the smoking flax, but to preach glad tidings to the poor, to heal the broken-hearted, and to grant forgiveness of sins to all the captives."

~~ MARTIN LUTHER

Afterward

About the Author: Charlie Jones and his wife, Ruth began Peculiar People, a theatrical touring ministry, sixteen years ago and have been accidentally encountering God's grace though their travels ever since. Their ramblin' SUV could be called an incubator of Peculiar Favor as God continues to pry open their stubborn hearts through all manner of circumstances–the good, bad and the ugly…you know who you are.

Contact the author:
Charlie Jones
PO Box 661646
Franklin, TN 37068
charlie@peculiarpeople.com

Order books through your local bookstore or on the World Wide Web:
www.peculiarpeople.com
Or by phone at:
(615)595-8782

Volume discounts available!!! Check it out!

Booking information for Peculiar People contact:
Curtis Stoneburger
(615)595-8782
curtis@peculiarpeople.com